Self-made women : twelve of America's le
338 JEN   10 99

Jennings, Diane.
Northampt

W9-BPM-276

Self–Made Women

Self-Made Women

TWELVE OF AMERICA'S LEADING ENTREPRENEURS TALK ABOUT SUCCESS, SELF-IMAGE, AND THE SUPERWOMAN

Diane Jennings

THE RONALD J. DARBY LIBRARY
Northampton High School

MR   '88

WITHDRAWN

TAYLOR PUBLISHING COMPANY • DALLAS

338
JEN

Copyright © 1987 by Diane Jennings

All rights reserved. No part of
this publication may be reproduced
in any form, or by any means, without
permission in writing from the publisher.

Library of Congress Cataloging-in-Publication Data

Jennings, Diane.
    Self-made women : twelve of America's leading en-
trepreneurial women talk about success, self-image, and
the superwoman / Diane Jennings.
        p.   cm.
    Bibliography: p.
    ISBN 0-87833-550-1 : $9.95
    1. Women in business.   2. Success in business.   I. Title.
HD6054.3.J46   1987
338'.04'088042—dc19   87-16104
                                                         CIP

Printed in the United States of America

9 8 7 6 5 4 3 2 1

To Mom, Dad, and Kay:
who never laughed when I said I wanted to write,
and who have always been there

Acknowledgments

Despite the popular picture of the writer as a solo artist, in the case of *Self-Made Women* nothing could be less accurate. This book is the result of the inspiration and cooperation of numerous people, who do not have the privilege I do of seeing their name in print.

My gratitude goes to Sue Goldstein, who first recognized the need for a book on entrepreneurial women; to Bobby Frese of Taylor Publishing, who recommended me as the writer for the project; to Christine Caperton, the original editor who helped formulate the idea in the early stages; and to Dominique Gioia of Taylor Publishing, who trusted me enough to give me the freedom I needed midway through the project, and who was there at the end to provide encouragement, suggestions, and much needed perspective.

In addition, the women who agreed to be interviewed for this book deserve a special vote of thanks. They are all extremely busy women who took time out of their hectic schedules to talk about their experiences.

But finally, this book would never have made it to press without another special group of people: those who listened and provided encouraging words and constructive criticism when I needed it most. To my sister, Kay Jennings, to my parents, Ken and Norma Jennings, and to my friend and colleague, Marty Primeau, my heartfelt gratitude.

D.L.J.

Contents

Self-Made Women

__ AUTHOR'S FOREWORD __

A unique movement is sweeping 1980s America, and this book is about the people leading that movement: entrepreneurial women. They have become contemporary heroines in a world more accustomed to heroes.

Casual observers may have noticed friends and neighbors starting their own businesses in recent years, at an unprecedented rate. Today's entrepreneur may be the man who occupied the next cubicle at the office and left a long-time job with an established company to strike out on his own; or it may be the woman next door who decided to rejoin the business world for the first time in years by employing herself.

Just as the 1970s was the decade of the managerial personality, when corporate climbing was honed to a fine art, and the position of supervising others within the corporate framework was hallowed, so the 1980s has become the decade of the entrepreneur. The corporate climber has been pushed aside in favor of the self-starter who begins his or her own business: the entrepreneur.

"Entrepreneur" may have become the hot new buzzword of the '80s, as a quick glance at the contents of any newsstand will prove, but it is no passing fad. Not only are more Americans starting new businesses than have done so in the past, but, if business school activities are any indication, a groundwork is being laid to foster even more entrepreneurs in the future. Previously, business administration programs rarely studied the genre, but today there are hundreds of curricula offering highly popular courses in entrepreneurship. In addition, the media, particularly in business magazines, newspapers, and television, have placed those who start their own companies on pedestals previously reserved for the explorers and conquerors of yesteryear.

In the United States today, the term "entrepreneur" has taken on a meaning significantly different from its original definition. The word first appeared in the French language in the early sixteenth century, when it referred to men engaged in leading military expeditions. In later centuries the term came to be associated with those who took the lead in pursuit of business, not military, risks.

According to Webster, entrepreneurs are those who "organize and manage a business undertaking, assuming the risk for the sake of profit."

Adulation for risk takers is nothing new. Since the dawn of time, the less adventurous have admired those who sauntered fearlessly into the unknown, whether it be across an uncharted ocean or into the wilds of a new continent. In today's increasingly mass produced, cookie-cutter society, arenas for risk taking are becoming harder and harder to find, so risk takers are lauded more than ever. In contemporary society even highly creative individuals are often confined to nondescript corporate cubbyholes, hemmed in by countless rules and regulations that stamp out individualism while proffering the carrot of security. Those who turn away from the carrot and strike out on their own in search of unknown reward, those who gamble on themselves and run the risk of failure—entrepreneurs—have been raised to mythical proportions. For many, these contemporary risk takers are tackling the only frontier available—business. Because entrepreneurs *act*, while others wisely weigh the pros and cons, because they *do*, while others talk, they have become the heroes of contemporary times.

Entrepreneurs may not leap buildings in a single bound or rescue people in distress, but they break the velvet chains of the corporate culture just as convincingly as legendary heroes. For taking risks and creating new businesses, even industries, where none existed before, entrepreneurs are invariably described in glowing terms, comparing them, often accurately, to those who walk a tightrope with no safety net.

Risk taking has traditionally been considered to be a male trait; consequently, heroes have historically been men. That perception still persists to some extent today. Despite rapid changes in the lifestyle of women in recent decades, the so-called "weaker" sex is still perceived as security, not risk, oriented. There have been notable exceptions through the years of course, but traditionally speaking, women are the ones who stayed behind and tended home and hearth, while members of the opposite, so-called "stronger" sex sallied forth to risk life and limb in serving as provider.

Historically, the business world has been a masculine domain. Though there have been marked changes in the business world in recent years as women have joined the work force in record numbers, no one can honestly contend that today women call the shots there.

For those reasons—the supposed female aversion to risk taking, and the relative unfamiliarity of women with the business world—the fact that the wave of entrepreneurism enveloping the United States is being led by women is an intriguing paradox. Common sense dictates that any such movement would be led by men, those who traditionally take risks and those who dominate the business world. But statistics overwhelmingly prove otherwise:

- In 1985, 3.6 million women operated their own businesses, accounting for more than $100 billion of the gross national product that year.
- Women business owners today account for a quarter of small businesses in the United States, and that number is expected to double by the turn of the century.
- Women are starting these businesses at more than twice the rate of men. From 1977 to 1983, the number of women-owned businesses increased annually by

9.4 percent while the increase in men-owned businesses rose by 4.3 percent.

Though I am a working woman and a journalist with more
than a passing interest in business, I found these statistics
surprising. Like most people, I am not by nature a risk
taker. I want to know where my next paycheck is coming
from, what the amount will be, and when it is due. So
the idea of talking with women who are willing to and
successful at taking risks, against awesome odds, was
compelling.

The implied contradiction of the term "entrepreneurial
women" is particularly intriguing, and as I researched the
topic I became more and more curious about the stories
behind the statistics. What, for example, motivated ladies
like cosmetics magnate Mary Kay Ash, who started Mary
Kay Cosmetics in 1963 with a $5,000 investment in un-
known formulations, assorted jars, and used office equip-
ment? Today she oversees a company with more than
100,000 sales associates, a volume in 1984 of approximately $278 million, and numerous manufacturing, ware-
house, and office facilities.

Or cookie queen Debbi Fields, who at the tender age of
twenty started selling homemade chocolate chip cookies
out of one store, and today heads up Mrs. Fields Cookies, an
organization with 350 stores that grossed $87 million in
1986.

Or mail order mogul Lillian Katz, who started selling
monogrammed accessories in 1951 through an ad in a teen
magazine and now runs the Lillian Vernon Corporation,
which in 1986 posted sales of $135 million sold through 81
million catalogs.

Or computer whiz Sandra Kurtzig, who in 1972 started
ASK Computer Systems Inc. with a desk, a file cabinet, and
a shoe box to hold the profits, and now boasts a company
with sales of approximately $76 million.

These women have built, and continue to run large corporations that place them among the most successful business executives, male or female, in the country. Their particular stories interested me because, while women are starting businesses faster than men, there are indications that the majority of those businesses do not grow as fast, or as large, as those started by their male counterparts. Some business watchers argue that women are more "self-employed" than "entrepreneurial," for several reasons. For instance, according to government statistics:

- Women-owned businesses make up one quarter of small businesses today, but those businesses accounted for only 10.2 percent of all business receipts, in 1982.
- Women-owned firms with paid employees accounted for only 10.8 percent of the total number of women-owned businesses in 1982, and of the approximately three million women-owned businesses in 1982, only 668 had 100 or more employees.
- Fifty-one percent of the women-owned firms had gross receipts of less than $5,000.

Some people theorize that most women-owned businesses start small and stay small because women don't have the desire or the drive to build major business empires. They are, in theory, content to be supplemental income earners, with "second bedroom businesses," (so dubbed because that's where the "company" is usually headquartered in the beginning).

Faced with both sets of statistics, those that showed women are starting their own businesses at a record pace, and those that indicate those companies may not be major factors in the overall business scheme, I began to wonder what set the super successful women entrepreneurs apart from not only their male counterparts, but also the majority of self-employed women. Though business schools are now paying attention to entrepreneurism as a field of study, it is such a new discipline that those who practice it are still shrouded in mystery. By talking to those who are successful entrepreneurs, I thought it might be possible to lift that shroud and shed some light on what makes a successful entrepreneurial woman. What motivated them to start their own businesses in the first place? Have they always been ambitious? Did they start and operate their businesses differently than men do? Why did their companies grow past the second bedroom stage and are they atypical of their gender? How did they handle the additional challenges and responsibilities which make business different for women?

Women such as Ash, Fields, Katz, and Kurtzig, may have started their businesses as small operations, but the companies didn't stay that way. They are not only leaders among entrepreneurial women, but also leaders in the business world as a whole. These women started businesses long before self-employment became widespread, and moved them out of the second bedroom and onto Wall Street and the financial pages.

Their achievements are even more impressive when considered in light of their gender. As women, they represent a minority faction who made it to the top without the benefit of being "one of the boys." In addition to facing the usual gargantuan headaches associated with starting a new business, they shouldered the added burden of being different from the majority of players in the game. There may be more women in the work force than ever before, totalling approximately 49 million, and there may be more women running their own businesses, but the board rooms and the conference rooms are still undeniably masculine domains. Ninety-eight percent of respondents surveyed for a 1986 executive profile conducted by Korn/Ferry International, an executive search firm, were men. The percentage of women in senior executive positions has increased, the study notes, from less than one percent in 1979, to 2 percent in 1986. But despite the increase, executive women in senior positions are still few and far between.

Those statistics made the subject of successful entrepreneurial women even more fascinating for me because not only have these women embarked on an upward climb to reach a level attained by only a handful, but they've done it by making their own mountain. Like successful entrepreneurs of either sex, these women saw a need and created a way to meet it, but whether it was a new type of cookie or a new type of marketing, coming up with a needed product was child's play compared to the obstacles they encountered when it came to presenting and executing their ideas. Like most entrepreneurs, these women heard their share of naysayers and doomsday prophets when starting out. But other barriers far more formidable than discouraging words or market studies faced them. Some of them encountered legal discrimination, such as the laws that made it impossible for a woman to secure a loan without her husband's consent. When Dallasite Paula Stringer opened her first real estate office in 1961 for instance, she had to go to court to have her "disabilities removed," by swearing to a judge that she, and not her spouse, would be responsible for her debts. Others merely ran up against traditional prejudices, such as colleagues who treated their businesses as hobbies, not serious ventures.

In addition, many women-owned businesses are started with little capital and even less formal education or practical experience. Diane Seelye Johnson, of Central Pipe & Supply, an oil field supply company, remembers starting the company by sitting on the bed in her bathrobe dialing general information to find telephone numbers for state sales tax offices. "I said, 'I don't know what I'm doing,'" she recalls, "'but we're starting a new business.'" Lillian Katz began Lillian Vernon Corporation with $2,000 in wedding gift money, while realtor Ellen Terry not only didn't have any experience or cash to tide her over when she embarked on a real estate career, she faced huge debts, accrued unwittingly during her marriage.

Women who could not only survive, but flourish, in the face of such large and small adversities must, I thought, have something in common, some background, some experience, some personality trait, that make them not only willing, but tremendously successful risk takers.

In a larger sense, my preliminary research indicated that the increase in women-owned businesses is changing the way America lives and works. As more and more women open their own companies, they become a business force to be reckoned with, not merely capable hands or minds to fill vacant positions. And as they become more of a business force, and less of supplemental income earners, their status in the community as a whole, and in their homes in particular, can't help but change radically. The difference for instance between being part of a staff of hundreds, and being responsible for the very existence, not to mention the maintenance of that staff, is monumental. The responsibility that accompanies a top executive position affects the way people conduct themselves, and the way they deal with others, at the office and at home. More and more women are finding themselves in these positions, in places they haven't been before, and where the rest of the world is not used to finding them. In the end, the trend to entrepreneurism among women will affect not only the women who are themselves directly involved, or their immediate environment, but the business world as a whole.

When I decided to write this book, I wanted *Self-Made Women* to include the most successful entrepreneurial women in the country. Most women-owned businesses are small enterprises today, but I wanted to talk to those women with proven track records, those who are successful by anyone's executive yardstick. I wanted the group to be a diverse one, with women from different professions, different geographic regions, and different generations, so that if there were any common characteristics to be found, they would be easily identifiable.

I did not want to talk to these women about business tips and techniques, such as where to go to obtain financing or how to set up a payroll system. There are dozens of business primers available to fill that need. And I did not want to talk to business analysts and psychologists about their observations on what motivates and makes these women successful. *Self-Made Women* is not intended as a business reference work, a statistical survey of hundreds of women, with the opinions of detached third party observers offering hard and fast conclusions. It is intended to offer an opportunity to listen to these women talk about themselves, about where they came from and how they rose to the executive suite of their own major company, a feat rarely achieved by members of either sex. It is meant to look at a new breed of business person, to show what these women are like. *Self-Made Women* offers the stories, opinions, and attitudes of a dozen of the top entrepreneurial women in the country, which considering the power these women wield in business circles around the country, should be of interest to everyone, male or female.

The search for entrepreneurial women superstars took me from New York to California and back again, with several stops in between. The only criteria for inclusion were staying power, significant company size, self-made financial success, and solid reputation. Many of these women are members of the prestigious Committee of 200, a national business organization consisting of women who are considered to be leaders and risk takers in their industry. Others are ranked repeatedly on the annual *Savvy 60* list of top U.S. businesses run by women. But all are counted among the best in their respective businesses.

The search turned up a fascinating, diverse group of women, with insightful stories to tell of their climb to the top of the business world, and what the view is like from that exalted position. Interviewees who graciously and generously gave of their time for this book include: Mary Kay Ash, Debbi Fields, Cathy Guisewite, Diane Seelye Johnson, Lillian Katz, Georgette Klinger, Kay Koplovitz, Sandra Kurtzig, Faith Popcorn, Paula Stringer, Ellen Terry and Louise Vigoda.

Half of these women work in industries generally regarded as "feminine," including Mary Kay Ash (cosmetics), Debbi Fields (cookies), Lillian Katz (mail order shopping), Paula Stringer (real estate sales), Ellen Terry (real estate sales), and Georgette Klinger (cosmetics). The other half represent less typically female fields, including Sandra Kurtzig (computer software), Diane Seelye Johnson (oil field supply), Kay Koplovitz (cable television), Faith Popcorn (marketing), Louise Vigoda (real estate development), and Cathy Guisewite (cartoonist). The inclusion of Guisewite may puzzle some readers because as the creator of the comic strip "Cathy," she does not run a "company" as such. Yet she has achieved international success in a field dominated by men, and her cartoon character, Cathy, has also become a symbolic spokeswoman for women of the '80s. To me, Guisewite represents entrepreneurism in the truest sense of the word, because on a daily basis, she faces the same risk as any other entrepreneurial woman: public acceptance of her product.

On the surface, this varied group of women appear to have little in common. They range in age from as young as 30 years old to well past the retirement stage. Some come from small families, others have numerous brothers and sisters. Though all are financially successful today, they came from varying socioeconomic backgrounds. They live in big cities like New York, as well as smaller towns like Park City, Utah. Some have earned several college degrees, others have none. Some are married, some are single. Some have children, some don't. Some are physically imposing, others are diminutive. None is a carbon copy of another, and they are undoubtedly more different than they are alike.

At first glance, the only thing they seem to share is a large measure of success, but beyond that, hours of interviews showed that many of them do share numerous characteristics in certain areas. Many of their traits, thoughts, and opinions may be as surprising to others as they were to me. It was not my intent to place these women in the role of spokespersons and this book was not written to present any unarguable conclusions. Though it would be fascinating to try, it would be impossible to gather these twelve women under one roof and have them agree completely on any subject. They may indeed be surprised to see themselves as I see them in these pages, because if I learned anything from these interviews, it is that entrepreneurial women are not analytical about their own success. They are marked by a "can-do" spirit, as opposed to the more analytical "let's talk" attitude. For that reason, many of them were uncomfortable analyzing their success because it goes against their natural inclination toward action, not introspection. They generally handled such requests graciously and with good humor, and I am especially appreciative of the time they took to cooperate and examine their motives and acts. Accordingly, it must be emphasized that any conclusions are my own, culled from hours of conversations with these women on many topics.

The primary reason for writing *Self-Made Women* was to stimulate thought about what makes a successful entrepreneurial woman. It offers readers the opportunity to look at a dozen of the most successful women in the country, listen to their stories, and I hope, discover what makes them tick. Perhaps it will also afford readers a chance to look within themselves and see what entrepreneurial characteristics they may or may not possess.

Readers who do take a close look at these entrepreneurial women will, I think, come to many of the same conclusions I did, including the notion that there is indeed something unique about them. They are possessed of tremendous self-confidence, an energy and willingness to work hard, and a strong sense of femininity they are unwilling to sacrifice. In addition, they show an increasing resistance to the idea of having to choose between career and home in order to succeed.

In doing so, these women are unwittingly changing the world. Because of the way they conduct themselves in business, they are bringing a regard for the human aspects, as well as the bottom line, to the previously masculine domain known as the business world. In doing what men have done for generations—insisting on their right to *both* a successful professional life and a personal one, they are prioritizing what's important in human relationships and bringing a fresh perspective to both the American home and business world. They make it possible for women to see that they have the ability to dictate their own priorities.

Diane Jennings

Gamblers

*U*nlike movie stars, politicians, athletes or other contemporary American heroes, prominent business executives often toil in relative obscurity. They may be well known in corporate circles, on Wall Street, or to the business press, but chances are their company's name is more pervasive than their own.

Many of the women included in this book have been featured frequently in both general interest and business-oriented publications. They have been interviewed by the media and applauded by their peers at industry functions, but more than likely, most of them are still unknown to a general audience. To familiarize readers with these twelve women, who are well worth knowing, the following thumbnail sketches are presented. Familiarity with their stories and accomplishments may lend insight into the attitudes and opinions they express later in this book, but more importantly, knowing who these women are, where they came from, and what they've done may also provide inspiration to other women.

Mary Kay Ash   With her near flawless complexion and always perfectly coiffed hair, Mary Kay Ash undoubtedly looks younger than her years. But Ash never reveals how old she is, because she believes that "a women who tells her age will tell anything." Still, her lengthy track record, as the founder of one of the earliest and most successful woman-owned businesses in the country, proves her to be a pioneer among entrepreneurial women. Ash, who is a great-grandmother, is the chairman of the board of Mary Kay Cosmetics, a company that sells an extensive product line through home beauty shows, resulting in approximately $278 million in sales in 1984, the last year such figures were made public.

Ash started the Dallas based company in 1963, after retiring from a successful twenty-five year career in direct sales for companies such as Stanley Home Products and World Gift. She began Mary Kay Cosmetics, originally called Beauty by Mary Kay, after an attempt to write her memoirs evolved into a management plan for her dream company. Ash was inspired to start Mary Kay because she felt she had been denied numerous opportunities due to her sex, and she wanted to form a company that offered women unlimited potential in terms of both income and flexible hours.

Ash had personal experience with the problems many women faced because she became a single parent of three at a young age when her first marriage ended in divorce.

Hard work was nothing new to her, however. As the youngest of four children, Ash spent most of her childhood taking care of her invalid father while her mother worked to pay for necessities by managing a restaurant. During her marriage, Ash worked as a waitress in her mother's restaurant until she realized she had an ability to sell. Her successful sale of ten sets of child psychology books, in order to win a free set for herself, led to a job as a saleswoman for Stanley Home Products.

The home parties where Stanley products were sold enabled her to earn more money and yet be home when her children returned from school, even when raising her children alone. After a thirteen year career with Stanley, where she became a top salesperson, Ash joined another direct sales company, where she was named national training director.

In 1963, Ash, who had since remarried, retired from

direct selling, but quickly became bored. She decided to start her own company using a product she had encountered years before: skin care formulations discovered by a leather tanner. Ash planned to concentrate on sales while her husband ran the administrative end of the new business; but a month before opening the business, he died suddenly.

Against the advice of her lawyer and accountant, Ash decided to carry out her plans with the help of her then twenty-year-old son, Richard. Mary Kay Cosmetics began with 500 square feet of space and nine friends serving as beauty consultants. By the end of 1984, the company had major distribution centers around the country and more than 150,000 consultants located everywhere from Dallas to Australia.

Ash is widowed and lives in Dallas, Texas.

Debbi Fields

Debbi Fields is thirty years old, with cover girl looks and an infectious, exuberant cheerleader style personality. When she pulls her long hair back into a ponytail she admits she looks thirteen, but despite her deceptively youthful appearance, Fields is an entrepreneurial veteran, having started her phenomenally successful cookie company at the age of twenty.

Mrs. Fields Cookies began in 1977, when Fields borrowed $50,000 with the help of her husband, and opened a store called Mrs. Fields Chocolate Chippery in Palo Alto, California. Despite the popularity of her cookies among friends, no one gave her commercial venture much chance of succeeding. Fields' cookies were soft, chewy, and warm, and research had shown that the public preferred a crispy, cold cookie. When customers were at first reluctant to buy the cookies, Fields handed out free samples. Sales followed, as did rapid expansion.

Fields is the youngest of five daughters in a family where the work ethic was stressed more than education. As a child she dreamed of a career where she could take care of people and make them feel better. She took some college courses and toyed with the idea of becoming a psychiatrist, but decided she'd rather make people happy by producing the chocolate chip cookies her friends and family raved about. That desire to make people smile is the main impetus behind Mrs. Fields Cookies, which has become one of the fastest growing women-owned businesses in the country.

By 1987, Mrs. Fields, now headquartered in Park City, Utah, had 350 stores in twenty-eight states as well as shops in Hong Kong, Japan, Australia, Canada, and England.

In addition to her duties as president of Mrs. Fields, Fields is married and the mother of three daughters.

Cathy Guisewite   Cathy Guisewite may not be a household name, but her cartoon character, Cathy, is a familiar face and figure to millions of newspaper readers. The Cathy character, which features its namesake's long brown hair and broad smile, evolved from early drawings contained in Guisewite's letters to her parents. The early, simple pictures illustrated the trials and tribulations Guisewite experienced as a Detroit advertising executive. When she submitted her drawings, at her mother's insistence, to a comic strip syndicate in 1976, Guisewite was immediately offered a contract.

Today, "Cathy" appears in more than 400 newspapers in the U.S. and thirteen foreign countries and is avidly followed by 70 million daily readers who identify with her successes, failures, and constant quandries. Her likeness also adorns more than 150 products and merchandise, and Guisewite has compiled numerous best-selling books. In addition, "Cathy" has been the basis of a live comedy show on network television.

Guisewite is the second of three daughters. She is a graduate of the University of Michigan, where she majored in English. Today, she makes her home in Los Angeles, California. She is thirty-six years old and single.

Diane Seelye Johnson　　When Diane Seelye Johnson, fifty-three, was growing up in Colorado there weren't many women in the general work force, much less in the oil field supply business. There still aren't many women in that industry, so as cofounder and executive vice president of Central Pipe & Supply, she is extremely visible.

Johnson didn't aspire to working in the oil field supply business, but arrived there after reentering the work force. Working first as an x-ray technician, then at various odd jobs as she followed her husband through several professional transfers, she left the business world for several years to start their family of three children.

When her two sons and daughter were all enrolled in school, Johnson decided to return to the classroom as well, going to college at age thirty-eight. After earning a degree in accounting, she opted to start an oil field supply company with her husband in 1975. He knew the field well from the sales viewpoint, but Johnson put her accounting education to work, which, interestingly enough, reversed the roles in the typical gender division of business duties. Though business has dropped with the economic problems of the oil industry, in 1984 Central Pipe & Supply hit a record volume of $72 million. 1986 sales totalled $20 million.

Johnson is married and lives in Houston, Texas.

Lillian Katz　　In 1986, 81 million brightly colored catalogs featuring everything from puzzles to tool caddies were mailed out under the name of Lillian Vernon. There is no Lillian Vernon as such, but there most definitely is a person behind the name, in the form of Lillian Katz. The energetic, sixty-year-old, chief executive officer at Lillian Vernon Corporation is a legend in mail order shopping.

Katz started Lillian Vernon in Mount Vernon, New York, in 1951 while awaiting the birth of her first child. She began the company by investing $2,000 of wedding gift money in a supply of belts and handbags, and in an ad in a teen magazine.

That initial investment resulted in a return of $16,000. Today Lillian Vernon Corporation boasts a volume of $135 million and maintains its own manufacturing division, retail outlet, and buying offices in Europe and the Orient.

Katz was born in Germany and lived in Holland before moving to New York at age ten. She studied psychology at New York University. Divorced and remarried, she is the mother of two sons.

Georgette Klinger

Georgette Klinger started advocating good skin care in the 1940s, before it became big business. Today she is considered one of the deans of skin care, with seven Georgette Klinger salons spread across the country from Beverly Hills to New York.

Klinger has made her reputation as an American businesswoman, but her European heritage is still very much evident, from her attitudes to her accent. Klinger was the only daughter of four children born to an affluent Czechoslovakian family. At age eighteen, she won a local beauty contest and received a makeup kit as a prize. Instead of enhancing her beauty however, the makeup caused a bad case of acne and awakened Klinger's interest in skin care. She sought help in Budapest, a city known for its skin care experts. There, she became fascinated with the subject and ended up studying it herself.

After marrying at twenty-one, Klinger found herself bored. She decided to open a skin care salon in her own town, in partnership with a local doctor. That venture was left behind however, when she fled Europe at the start of World War II. Klinger relocated to New York, where she opened another salon in 1940. Though others advised her against it, pointing out that supplies were hard to come by in a wartime economy, she managed to make a success of the salon.

When her marriage ended in divorce, Klinger depended on the salon to make a living. She later remarried and had a daughter, but kept the salon operating. Through the years the salon garnered a loyal clientele, and in 1970 Klinger opened a second location in Beverly Hills. Today she presides over seven salons and continues to work in researching new products.

She is widowed and lives in New York.

Kay Koplovitz
Kay Koplovitz loves negotiating deals, and as president and chief executive officer of USA Network, she's obviously good at it. Her track record with the first advertiser-supported basic cable service in the U.S. is impressive, including successful deals for the first national cable television agreements with major league baseball, the National Basketball Association, and the National Hockey League.

Koplovitz is the middle of three children raised in Milwaukee. She graduated from the University of Wisconsin with a bachelor's degree in science and communication in 1967, followed by a master's degree in communication from Michigan State University. After stints as a television producer, and positions in various areas of communications, she formed her own public relations and communications management firm.

In 1980, Koplovitz was asked to start another new company, USA Network, which was later acquired by Time Inc., Paramount Pictures Corporation, and MCA Inc. At USA, Koplovitz has overseen the company's shift from sports programming to general entertainment and watched it grow into one of the most watched basic cable networks in the country. Today, USA Network boasts 8,500 affiliates and a viewing audience of more than 35 million.

Koplovitz is forty-one, married, and lives in New York.

Sandra Kurtzig   Women are still so unusual in high-tech fields that Sandra Kurtzig, chairman of ASK Computer Systems Inc., is considered something of a novelty. At one meeting a large, red heart was projected onto a screen behind her when she was introduced, a sort of respectful valentine for what she has accomplished in the highly competitive computer software industry.

Kurtzig, forty, started ASK, named for the initials of herself and her former husband, Ari, in 1972. After earning a bachelor's degree in math and chemistry from the University of California at Los Angeles, and a master's degree in aeronautical engineering from Stanford, she worked in the aerospace industry and for a business systems company. But when the Kurtzigs decided it was time to start a family, she left the corporate world for freelance work at home.

Freelance work quickly evolved into more than a full-time job however, as ASK developed a broad line of software tools designed to help customers manage numerous different business functions. In 1981, Kurtzig took ASK public. Today it is one of the fastest growing publicly held companies in the country, with sales of approximately $76 million in 1986.

Kurtzig lives in Palo Alto, California, is divorced, and the mother of two.

Faith Popcorn   Faith Popcorn's uncanny ability to forecast trends in American buying habits has made her a highly sought after marketing consultant. Her company, BrainReserve, a New York marketing consultancy firm, has been successfully predicting changing consumer tastes, from flashy cars to gourmet fast food since 1974.

Popcorn, forty, serves as chairman of the company she named because of her preference for "brainstorming" sessions. BrainReserve brings creative talent together with proven marketing strategies to develop new products, reposition established brands, and define new markets. Clients include everyone from Quaker Oats to Timex. Popcorn has won seven prestigious Clio awards, as well as other industry recognition.

Popcorn was born in New York but spent her early years in China. Her parents, both lawyers, moved back to New York when she was six. A summer job in advertising during college piqued her interest in the industry, and after earning an English degree from New York University, she worked for several different advertising agencies.

And yes, the last name of Popcorn is one of her clever marketing ideas. Born Faith Plotkin, she had the name change to Popcorn made legal, and concocted a tale about her Italian grandfather: Supposedly named Corne, he introduced himself as Papa Corne, to a U.S. immigration official who recorded it, literally, as Papacorne.

Popcorn is single and lives in New York.

Paula Stringer

Dallas is a city dominated by successful female realtors, and Paula Stringer was one of the first.

Stringer opened her first real estate agency with a friend in 1958. She had no business experience because she had dropped out of college to marry and raise a family, but she had been interested in real estate since childhood. As the oldest of two children in her family, she had often accompanied her father, a telephone company engineer, to look at potential investment property, so she had some background in land values and opportunities.

Three years after entering the real estate business, she opened an agency under her own name. Several years later she had built it into one of the largest in the city. By 1979, Paula Stringer Realtors had twenty offices in the Dallas-Fort Worth area, including residential, corporate and commercial offices with approximately 500 associates. That year Merrill Lynch bought the company, using it to launch their residential real estate business. After the sale Stringer remained as chairman of the board for four more years.

A mother of three, Stringer has been divorced and has remarried. She lives in Dallas, Texas.

Ellen Terry   Ellen Terry knew nothing about selling houses when she went to work for a Dallas real estate agency in 1976. She simply "bowed my neck and said I can do it."

Terry not only did it, she did it exceptionally well, becoming one of the firm's top saleswomen, locally and nationally. Two and one half years later, Terry opened an agency with two friends, then left that company in 1981 to start Ellen Terry Realtors. In the first four years of operation, Ellen Terry Realtors sold more than $400 million in volume.

Terry chose real estate as a career out of necessity. Her marriage to a banking executive ended in financial chaos, leaving her with a mountain of debts and responsibility for two children. She had earned a teaching degree from Southern Methodist University and taught physical education for five years, but went into real estate when she needed more income than an education career could provide.

Terry, forty-seven, has been so successful in motivating her staff to sell real estate that she has become a popular motivational speaker. Today the petite (four-feet-ten-inches) executive concentrates on the real estate business and travels around the country for speaking engagements.

She is divorced, and lives in Dallas, Texas.

Louise Vigoda   Louise Vigoda has a master's degree in psychology, but she has made her business reputation in real estate development. The fifty-seven-year-old businesswoman is the founder of Hera Investments, a property development and management company based in Denver.

Vigoda concentrated on being a physician's wife and mother of three, until she realized the need to make some outside investments for the sake of financial security. She started Hera twenty years ago as a part-time job, by buying and managing one property, then another, as different office building and retail opportunities became available. Today Hera oversees six commercial properties around the city and surrounding area.

Vigoda is the oldest of two children, who were adopted by their aunt after their mother's death. She studied psychology, philosophy, and sociology at Ohio State University.

Vigoda is married, the mother of three, and lives in Denver, Colorado.

Most of these women are energetic, goal-oriented achievers, perfectionists in everything they do. That sort of zealousness, whether it be Debbi Fields' insistence on personally testing batches of chocolate chips before they go into her cookies, or Mary Kay Ash confessing that even the cup towels in her linen closet have to be folded exactly so, seems natural to anyone who builds a company from nothing into a major business entity. Cathy Guisewite sums up the attitude of many of these women succinctly when she says, "I never think of doing anything in terms of middling."

Many of them also have tremendous self-confidence and an unshakable belief that they can do whatever they set their minds to. This positive self-image was usually instilled in them at one point or another by a close family member. For most, it was either or both of their parents; for Fields, it was her husband; for Faith Popcorn it was her grandparents. "My grandmother told me I could do anything I wanted, my grandfather swore to it . . ." Popcorn says. "I believed I could do anything I wanted to." Cartoonist Guisewite not only remembers being told she could be a great artist or writer, but also that her mother, not content to simply post her childish creative efforts on the family refrigerator, submitted her daughter's work to magazines for publication.

Those characteristics are perhaps what one would expect to find among the super successful, but other traits that many of these women exhibited are surprising.

For instance, many of these bright, attractive, self-confident women described themselves during childhood as loners. At age forty, Popcorn confesses that "what I really wanted more than anything else in the world was to belong. Nobody really asked me to belong." Fields still squirms uncomfortably at the memory of being elected homecoming queen and having to plead with someone to escort her to the festivities because she didn't have a date.

And despite their achievements, and their strong self-images, many of these women said they didn't have unusually high aspirations as children. Some of them wanted to be nurses or teachers, some wanted to pursue acting careers, others dreamed of being cowboys. For the most part however, they had only vague career goals, generally accompanying the assumption that they would marry and have children.

Equally astonishing is the number of these successful women, top executives of multi-million dollar companies, who said they fell into business by accident, and were surprised one day to find themselves heading up a major business entity. Few, if any, of these women started out with any sort of ultimate professional ambition. "My first goal was making it to lunch," says Sandra Kurtzig.

They were not motivated by dreams of great wealth or of making an indelible mark on the business world. Neither were the majority of them unhappy with life in the corporate world, as are many entrepreneurial men. Instead, these women struck out on their own simply because they craved greater flexibility, not as the result of any great master plan. Often they needed more open-ended hours because of their family responsibilities, and had nothing more grandiose in mind than a "second bedroom" business. (Ironically, most of them ended up working more hours than they ever imagined as their companies grew beyond their wildest dreams.) Kurtzig, for instance, began her computer software company in her apartment in order to rear her family and have some spending money. "I just wanted enough money to buy little things," she says of her original intent. "My husband was supporting me and I wanted to have something to do to keep my mind active when the kids were sleeping."

Also surprising was the fact that, despite the added difficulties being a woman in business often poses, generally these women consider their gender to be a benefit, not a disadvantage. Many of them have faced blatant and subtle prejudices, whether it be applying for a loan or being mistaken for clerical help instead of the chief executive officer. Still, for various reasons—perhaps just the fact that being different means being noticed—they have managed to turn their sex from a liability into an advantage. Kay Koplovitz, president and CEO of USA Network, chooses to view being different as a plus, not a minus. "If you go to a room full of fifty people having a meeting, if you are the only woman in there, I guarantee every one in that room will remember who you are," she says. In cable television, a field dominated by men, Koplovitz speaks from experience.

On one hand, given the ability of these women to turn their gender into an advantage, and the legal, societal, and economic prejudices many of them encountered on the other, it is also surprising how few of these women identify with the organized women's liberation movement. This is a group of strong, successful, businesswomen who have succeeded despite tremendous odds and disadvantages, yet most of them, while expressing appreciation for the progress brought about by the feminist movement, do not generally consider themselves part of it. Developer Louise Vigoda says she finds the term "feminist" limiting. "I believe that everyone has the right to develop to whatever extent their ability and desire takes them to, that it is not just women, that it's everybody," Vigoda says. She never supported the organized women's movement, she adds, "I detested the bra burning people, and those individuals. I was embarrassed by them."

Kurtzig is equally uncomfortable with the term "feminist." The word has negative connotations she says, adding that while she agrees with the idea of equal rights, she disagrees with the organized activity. "Women don't need to wave a banner of equality," Kurtzig explains. "I think if they're really equal and they're comfortable with the fact that they're equal, they don't need to go waving the banner. They need to just go and perform."

Gender may be a non-issue to most of these women personally, but they are not naive. They acknowledge reluctantly that their gender is still a factor for others. They would like simply to be part of the overall business world, and confess that they are weary of being identified as "women" entrepreneurs instead of simply "entrepreneurs." But at the same time they admit that women conduct business differently from their male counterparts. Intuition, sensitivity, and natural nurturing instincts, for instance, play a much larger role in their companies than in male dominated businesses.

"I've institutionalized my company in a nurturing

manner so people can learn from me," says Lillian Katz. "I try to teach them the broad picture, to show how to make a decision. I don't do it the way men do. I do not fight a battle that if the attack doesn't work that way, we'll go the other way. If you listen to a man plan a business plan, it sounds like a war plan, like Eisenhower and his generals. I don't have that same approach. It's very hard to explain these things. You do things the way you do and keep doing them."

These women also recognize that members of their sex are expected to cope with more outside responsibility than men. No one, they agree, ever asks male business executives how they manage to "have it all." Though there is an increasing rebellion against the idea of having to choose between family and business—successful men do not face that no-win proposition—most of them say women instinctively put their children first. "Mothers in the animal world take care of the baby more," explains Georgette Klinger. "It's natural. The other is learned."

But instead of bemoaning the burden of the extra responsibilities heaped on their sex, most of these women expend their energies coping with the situation, not trying to change it. The rallying cry of the turbulent '60s may have been "change," but in the fast-paced, career oriented '80s, it is "cope." The '80s "coping" approach differs drastically from the traditional attitude of the feminist movement, which advocated the need for change. Instead of bemoaning the idea of the do-it-all woman who sends the husband and kids off in the morning, goes to work looking stunning, puts in a full day at the office, stops by the gourmet grocery on her way home, whips up a tantalizing meal, keeps the house spotless, helps the kids with their homework, and still has time to devote to her husband, these women are trying to manage their time, prioritize, and perfect that juggling act. The important difference is in their acknowledgment of the fact that even with the household help many of them can and do afford, there are still times when they can't do it all. They have learned to let certain things slide when necessary and refuse to rake themselves over mental coals for it.

Their attitude represents a significant change: *they continue to try to be Superwomen, and they don't try to change that ideal, but they won't be defeated by it when the ideal isn't realized.* They accept it and do the best they can, refusing to criticize themselves if they fail, or praise themselves when they succeed.

"I just use the microwave more," says Debbi Fields, who married a traditional husband, who doesn't do household chores or assume child care responsibility for their three daughters. "And I don't want you to check my closets." She never debates the fairness of her extra responsibilities, Fields says. "There are so many things in life that aren't fair, that I never really question. Addressing the fact that it's not fair is not really going to change the situation."

But the most intriguing trait evidenced was the traditionally masculine trait of risk-taking, enhanced by a delightfully feminine twist. That twist comes from the uniquely feminine qualities women bring to their entrepreneurial ventures: intuition, flexibility, and high energy. These qualities result in the biggest twist of all: the *ability* to refuse to fail. Because of that refusal, they do not fear failure, because they don't recognize it.

These women don't see their foray into entrepreneurism as either foolhardy or courageous. Instead of acknowledging their steps outside the traditional role of protected wife or protected corporate employee as risky business, many of these women respond to the question of whether they feared failure with a puzzled stare. Their blank looks indicate that the idea never occurred to them.

For many of them, it didn't. These women talk of

opportunity, not chance; of excitement, not danger; of the risk for potential gain, not the possibility of failure.

"Failure never entered my mind," says Ellen Terry. Terry points to the cartoon behind her desk which shows a rabbit being pursued by a coyote. "Rabbit, you gonna make it?" inquires a passing farmer. "Man," replies the rabbit, "I *gotta* make it." She had no choice either, Terry says, so she didn't consider the possibility.

"I didn't know I was taking risks," echoes Ash. Twenty-three years after starting her company she sounds as if the notion is still foreign. "All I knew was I saw it as an opportunity . . . I decided it was going to work or else. I just never even thought about the fact that it would fail. That was not a possibility."

The willingness of these women to take a chance doesn't mean they don't consider themselves security oriented, many of them hasten to point out. They simply didn't consider relying on themselves a gamble.

"Everybody talks about entrepreneurs being risk takers," says Randy Fields, husband of Debbi, who she credits with helping her develop self-confidence. "They're not risk takers [in their own minds] . . . Ask an entrepreneur if his idea is going to work, and he says, 'Of course it will.'"

The feminine quality of intuition plays a key role, says Fields, who was initially skeptical of his wife's business venture. "The major feature of a good entrepreneur is terrific intuition. The other characteristic of an entrepreneur is self-confidence, an ability to take risks with the understanding there's no possibility of failure."

That attitude doesn't mean these women simply put their heads in the sand or close their eyes to what is going on around them. They do not ignore the possibility of failure nor do they delight in taking risks. *They simply don't perceive the presence of either, and thus feel no threat.*

The inability to perceive and be intimidated by the possibility of failure is a "mental defect," jokes Randy Fields.

"[Debbi] is the kind of person that on Christmas Eve would go shopping at the shopping center and instead of taking the first [parking] space that she finds, which is what I think most people would do, which is way in the back of the parking lot, she says, 'Oh no, there'll be one right in front of the door.' And she'll go get the one right in front of the door. It's irrational to imagine there is one right in front of the door," Fields says, "but it's always there."

"You do things from an enlightened self-interest," explains Diane Seelye Johnson. "There's no way I would put $2 on a horse at a racetrack. I don't know what the horse is going to do. I don't know what the jockey is going to do. I have no control over what they do . . . But if after looking at the possibilities, I can put two bucks some place else and take a chance on making that two bucks grow or losing it, and I have some control over it, at least enough control to make the decision. . . ." That's no gamble.

Though these characteristics, particularly the absence of a fear of failure, seem present in many of these women, one final trait of female entrepreneurs must also be pointed out: their distinct individualism. Many of these women, while happy to discuss their own experiences and opinions, were reluctant to speak for their sex as a whole. Many of them are also skeptical of finding any shared characteristics among entrepreneurial women.

Not all of these women were exceptional students or overly ambitious youngsters. They don't necessarily come from extraordinary parents or homes, and the backgrounds of these twelve remarkable women show they weren't much different from everyone else on the block. But they were willing to dream big and work hard to make their dreams come true. And for other women willing to do the same, there's plenty of room on the mountaintop to share the spectacular view.

Reason to Gamble

"I wasn't 'starting a company.' It was
$2,000 I bought a desk and a file cabinet
with. When I made $3,000, that was more
than $2,000."

*J*ust over ten years ago, Ellen Terry was hosting a
Junior League meeting at her Dallas home, when the
front doorbell rang. Expecting to greet a late arriving
member, she opened the door to find a man wearing me-
chanics' overalls.

"I'm here to pick up the keys to your Mercedes," he
told her. "The payments have not been made for a number
of months."

Protesting that he must be mistaken, she closed the
front door and stepped out onto the front porch. A tow
truck was parked in front of her home.

"There's got to be levity in every situation or we'd
go crazy," Terry says, laughing now at the memory. "My
thought was, 'The Junior League is in my living room. When
you're a member of the Junior League, nothing like this can
happen to you.'"

There was no mistake, and what Terry found out in
subsequent months was that not only were she and her
husband behind on the car payments, but they owed approximately $100,000 to the Internal Revenue Service for

unpaid taxes and penalties. In addition, many of their assets had been sold.

Terry was thirty-seven years old in 1976, the wife of a banking executive for a decade, and the mother of two children. The Terrys had a house in an affluent neighborhood, a Mercedes in the driveway, and their children were enrolled in private schools. Terry devoted her time to motherhood, volunteer work, and perfecting a competitive tennis game.

"I was living the carefree life of the Dallas housewife and the volunteer worker," the diminutive, dynamic Terry says. "I was kind of living the American dream, insulated by my protective bubble of the 'right' groups and the 'right' people."

But when the doorbell rang that day, the bubble burst.

The marriage, which Terry had always assumed would last forever, fell apart quickly as she discovered her life was not what she thought it was.

The Terrys divorced, and she was forced to fend for herself. The result was an extraordinarily successful career as an entrepreneur. First she sold her jewelry to friends and her clothes at a garage sale. The Mercedes was long gone, so she made do by borrowing cars from friends and relatives. Terry moved into a tiny apartment and sent her children to live temporarily with their grandparents.

Before her marriage, Terry had worked as a physical education teacher, but because of the limited earnings potential, and the prospect of living in a child's world around the clock, she had no desire to return to the classroom. Instead she sought employment with no other guideline than a desire to work in a people-oriented field. Terry went to work for a travel agency, but the $12,000 annual salary soon proved too small. "I realized very quickly that [salary] was not going to allow me the income to bring my kids back to me and live any semblance of a comfortable lifestyle," Terry says.

Though she didn't have any background in sales and knew nothing about selling houses, Terry decided to go into real estate. "I wanted a job that didn't place a ceiling on the monetary income," she says. "I didn't care how many hours it took."

Terry enrolled in the necessary educational courses, convinced a real estate agency to hire her, and began spreading the word about her new career. Then one day, while sitting behind the wheel of a borrowed car at a traffic signal, she spotted a former student. Terry rolled down the window and said, "I'm getting ready to go into the real estate business. Do you know anybody looking for a house?" The former student replied that she might be in the market herself and told Terry to call her.

New colleagues had warned her to expect a six-month drought before making her first sale, but as soon as she passed the examination, Terry called her former student. The woman said she was still interested in buying a house— if she could find something in a certain price range.

"We don't want to spend a penny over $400,000," she explained.

"I picked myself up off the floor and said I thought maybe we had one or two things in inventory that inexpensive," Terry remembers, laughing.

Within thirty days she had sold her former student a house. The people selling that home then asked Terry to find one for them as well, and within forty-five days Terry earned $12,000—the equivalent of a year's work at the travel agency.

Two and a half years later, Terry was the firm's top ranked salesperson statewide and number two in the country. Shortly after that she left the agency to start an office with two friends. Then in 1981 she founded her own company, Ellen Terry Realtors.

In the first four years of operation, Ellen Terry Realtors sold more than $400 million in property.

*   *   *

If adversity in the form of "sheer financial devastation" hadn't burst her bubble, Ellen Terry says she would never have gone into business for herself. Other entrepreneurial women say it was also circumstance that provided the final motivational push toward self-employment, though the situation was rarely so dire as the one Terry faced. For some their motivation was the desire to do something different; for others it was the need for flexible hours; and for others it was a way of earning extra income. Few of these women, however, felt any burning desire or internal impulsion to be her own boss. But though they went into business for different reasons, and were often surprised to find themselves heading up major companies, these women are ambitious, not necessarily for money, power, or prestige, but for challenge. Any entrepreneurial bent or ability they were born with was developed and guided, often unconsciously, through circumstances and experience, until it reached fruition by rising to the challenge of entrepreneurship. But without circumstances to push them into it, many of them say they probably would never have become entrepreneurs.

Louise Vigoda, for instance, was, and is, the happily married wife of a physician and the mother of three. Though her husband earned a more than adequate salary, Vigoda decided to go to work when she saw a friend's life fall apart, not through divorce, but through death. "There's a lot to be said for the swift kick in the pants," Vigoda says. "I had the swift kick in the pants when my friend's husband died."

The friend was also the wife of a doctor. "The day he died," Vigoda says, "was the day the money stopped. Her husband was never interested in investments, nor was mine." Her friend fell apart, Vigoda remembers. "She became an emotional basket case and a financial basket case. She had three children, exactly the same age as my three children. I said, 'That could happen to me, because my husband is interested only in medicine.' We had no investments. The money sat in a savings account in a bank. I said, 'My God, that could be me. I've got to do something.'"

What Vigoda did was start looking for real estate investments. It took her two years to find one she liked. Once she found it, she took a small office and began managing the building she'd purchased. When she saw another piece of property undergoing foreclosure proceedings across the street, she took over that one. The business gradually grew.

Other entrepreneurial women have less worrisome reasons than divorce or death for going into business. For some it was a matter of bumping up against the "glass ceiling," that level of senior management in the male dominated corporate world that women reach and seem unable to go beyond. "Glass ceiling" is the term that has been coined for the point at which women "top out" in management. Their positions at this point are high enough to offer a tantalizing view into the board room, but because of traditional sexist prejudices, there is little hope of being asked to take a seat there. Some women, like Mary Kay Ash, open their own businesses to avoid that ceiling, creating a company where there are no prejudices to erect such barriers.

Ash started Mary Kay Cosmetics after becoming frustrated at the treatment she received in male-dominated companies. When she worked for various direct selling organizations in the 1950s, women "walked three paces behind the boss," she says. She became a top saleswoman, but often spent months on the road training men to do the same job she did, only to return home to find the male trainee had become her supervisor.

"Suddenly, he was telling me what to do, and I'm the one who taught him what to do," Ash says. "I figured if I could teach him what to do, how come I couldn't do the job? The man who owned the company I was with thought only a man could be a sales manager. So he called me a 'national training director' and paid me half as much."

The working world offers improved opportunities for women today, but Ash doesn't think it's changed dramatically. "They're still reaching that glass ceiling, and there's nothing they can do about it," she says. "We've been 'token' this and 'token' that for so doggone long, that's where we are. When you get tokened out, you start your own business."

Most of these women who worked in the corporate world before opening their own venture weren't as dissatisfied as Ash. Some often professed to having been content with their jobs and unaware of or undisturbed by the glass ceiling. Ironically, it is men who typically go into business for themselves because they are unhappy in the corporate world. The study of entrepreneurs is a relatively new one, and almost all surveys on the subject are dominated by male respondents. Such studies often indicate that most entrepreneurs become self-employed because they are unhappy with their career paths or dissatisfied with the corporate world. Though these women were aware of the barriers they faced, most of them said that when they worked they were not particularly frustrated by them, and for the most part enjoyed corporate life. Those who sought self-employment out of frustration tend to be those who worked solely as wives and mothers. It was the traditional housewife role that left Georgette Klinger and Diane Seelye Johnson feeling unchallenged and looking for something more.

"I decided I wanted to do something [because] I was bored to death with my life," says Klinger. She and her husband, an international lawyer, were living in her native Czechoslovakia at the time. "The clique was doctors' and lawyers' wives," Klinger says. "We'd meet for tea every afternoon. That was the thing to do. When each of us left, it was, 'Did you see what she ordered?' 'Did you see her hair?' or 'How can she live with this man?' or something. It was terrible. After a while, I had enough."

Klinger talked to her husband about her frustration. "I said, look this cannot go on," she remembers. "That life I do not want. I have to do something." She mentioned her desire to open a skin care salon, only to encounter fierce family opposition. Her in-laws were especially opposed she says, protesting that it would look as if her husband could not support her. Finally Klinger took her mother-in-law to visit the places where she had studied, and explained the profession she wanted to enter. They gave their consent, if not their approval.

But by far, one of the most common reasons cited by these women for going into business for themselves was not dissatisfaction in the home or the corporation. It was a more positive and down-to-earth motive: the desire to make a little extra money in a job with flexible hours.

That's one of the main reasons Mary Kay Cosmetics has been so successful. The direct sales through home parties method fulfilled two desires of modern women at the same time: to make money and to have flexible hours, enabling them to be home with their children. Those are primary motivations for many entrepreneurial women, but are rarely cited by men as a reason for seeking self-employment.

Lillian Katz started what is now the Lillian Vernon Corporation in 1951 when she was pregnant for the first time. She wanted more comforts than she and her husband could afford on his salary. "We did not, in my evaluation, have enough to live on," she says, "to have an apartment, have a child, have a car. I wanted household help, so there was not anything else to do but go to work."

Katz took $2,000 in wedding gift money, selected two items from her father's leather goods manufacturing inventory, and placed an ad for personalized handbags and belts in a teen magazine. The ad generated $16,000 in sales, and thirty-five years later, Lillian Vernon, the company named for herself and Mount Vernon, New York, where it is headquartered, is an established mail order firm, international in scope.

Though she planned to make a success of her business, Katz admits she didn't expect to become a mail order legend. "I woke up one day and said, 'I have a $130 million business.'"

Like Katz, many of these women have found themselves surprised at the extent of their success. "I hoped to make enough to pay the bills," says Ash. "But I had no idea we would ever get past Waxahachie [Texas]."

That was about the extent of Sandra Kurtzig's hopes when she started ASK Computer Systems Inc. "It wasn't 'starting a company,'" Kurtzig says. "It was $2,000 I bought a desk and a file cabinet with. When I made $3,000 that was more than $2,000."

For others wondering if they too can become successful entrepreneurs, one of the most fascinating and reassuring aspects of the phenomenal success these women have attained is the fact that few, if any of them, had a long-range master plan or burning desire to make their mark on the business world. They didn't set out to build a company or become business leaders, they merely wanted an improved quality of life, in terms of money and time. The way they started their now legendary businesses is the way most women start out: on a personal, limited scale, with realistic goals, such as making some money and being able to control their schedules.

This is also the way many women-owned businesses remain. Observers of the trend to entrepreneurship among women tend to dismiss the movement for this reason, drawing a sharp distinction between self-employment and entrepreneurship. Self-employment, they point out, does not create a business as such because there are no other workers involved. Entrepreneurism, on the other hand, involves the hiring of employees and significant financial activity. Using those definitions, statistics do indeed indicate that women tend more toward self-employment than entrepre-neurism at this early stage in their business history. But because self-employment was the original intent of most of these super-successful entrepreneurial women, one can't help but wonder how many Mary Kay Cosmetics, Lillian Vernon Corporations, Mrs. Fields Cookies, and ASK Computer Systems Inc. are being nurtured in what appear today to be unimportant "second bedroom" businesses. There has been a far smaller group of entrepreneurial women in the past from which such success stories sprang, so it stands to reason with the increased number of women opening their own businesses, there can't help but be more and more major companies forming right now.

Those women who have already come through the per-ilous early years of business growth, worked too long and too hard, and are too smart to consider their extraordinary success luck. But many of them admit their successes were accidental, not planned. Most of their companies have elabo-rate, carefully orchestrated growth plans today, but few of them were begun with anything more long-term in mind than "making it through lunch," as Kurtzig says. None of them planned to become entrepreneurial leaders or to run multi-million dollar companies; most of them simply wanted something to do that offered flexibility and/or some added income.

The flexibility that holds so much appeal, and lures so many women into opening their own businesses, might seem to be a handicap in the corporate world. It may appear to be short-sightedness, a characteristic considered to be a weakness in companies that refer reverently to a proven track record, and speak confidently of the carefully plotted future they look forward to. But among entrepreneurs, flex-ibility is sometimes cited as a key to success, and is un-doubtedly a key to survival. An ability to adapt is critical, because entrepreneurial ventures by definition are pursued in uncharted waters. Given the unpredictability of new businesses, and the fact that entrepreneurs are more action-oriented than analytical, the ability to adapt and respond to situations as they arise is not only tolerable but desirable.

Kurtzig, now hailed as one of the country's most successful executives, freely admits her professional accomplishments were unplanned. "I fell into it," Kurtzig says. "When I finally woke up fourteen years later, I said, 'I started this as a part-time job so I could stay home with my kids—and the only thing I'm not doing is staying home with my kids.'"

The desire to earn money and stay home with the kids, that flexibility, also extends to the attitude these women take toward earning money. Traits that lead to success may be genderless, but motivations are often markedly different between the sexes. Women tend to aim for a little supplemental income, whereas men are typically much more focused on earning potential. Those tendencies on the part of both sexes are undoubtedly due in large part to social conditioning. Even with rapidly changing times, men are still raised with the expectation that they will be the primary breadwinner, and women, unless forced by unexpected circumstances, still tend to think of their careers as secondary or supplemental in terms of income.

"Most women don't think they're going to be their ultimate supporter," observes Cathy Guisewite, "and so I don't think money is the same motivation for women that it ever is for men, with a few exceptions."

Though none of these women portray themselves or come across as clinging vines or "husband hunters," most of them said that during their early years they expected to be taken care of financially through marriage. Many went to work for themselves because it fit their family responsibilities better than an outside job.

"I thought I was going to get married to a successful man, have three children, and stay by the swimming pool," says Louise Vigoda, noting that it was an assumption rather than an aspiration. "This is the way it was going to be."

"I suppose I hoped we would have that little white cottage with the picket fence and he would work and take care of me," says Ash, of her first marriage, which ended in divorce and pushed her into the business world with three children to support. "I suppose I thought that. It didn't work out that way at all."

That often mistaken assumption, that they will be taken care of instead of being caretakers, explains the reduced earnings expectations of entrepreneurial women within marriage. But in or out of marriage, tremendous wealth is simply not a primary motivation for most successful entrepreneurial women. Most of these women have become enviably rich now, but the challenge their work offers and job satisfaction still rank as their top goals.

"I don't think that [wealth] was a goal," says Paula Stringer, who started her real estate firm in 1961 as a way to expand her horizons beyond her roles as a wife and mother. The company did well from the beginning but really flourished after her divorce, when it became more of a financial necessity. Stringer later made a substantial profit when she sold the company to Merrill Lynch, but riches were never her primary motivation, she says. "That came with it, but it wasn't the number one goal. I think women are really less interested in making money. I think it's everything that goes with it they enjoy more," Stringer says. Other women agree. "The reason I worked was not because I needed the money," says Kurtzig. "And not because I needed to be a career woman, but because I really loved it. I worked and I did it because it was just the most exciting thing going. It was stimulating solving problems and seeing people use things I was developing and seeing them happy at it. It was exciting. Then we started making money, and that was amazing."

Money to many people is a measure of success, a way to keep track of how well an individual is doing in the game of big business. While these women like to be ahead in that game as much as anyone else, they generally do not suffer from a "never enough" mentality. For many of them, money is a means to an end, not the end itself. "Making money for the sake of security is more important to me," explains Ellen Terry, "than making money for the sake of making money. It's not to keep score."

People who seek financial success first do not good entrepreneurs make, some observers theorize, and that may explain the success of many of these women. These entrepreneurs are genuinely thrilled with their products and convinced that the world is a better place because of what they offer. They fret over quality and service, not only because of how it will impact the bottom line, but because their personal reputation is at stake. It is not simply a matter of good business, but personal pride that keeps them running frantically around the world in search of new merchandise, or spending countless hours in the research laboratory testing new products, or continuing to sample ingredients personally, long after their reputation and fortunes have been made. That's evidenced, at least in part, by the fact that many of these women have rejected lucrative offers to buy out their businesses, and some work well past what has traditionally been considered retirement age. These women are, for the most part, financially set for life; none really need to work for financial reward any longer. They do need to work for the pleasure they derive from it, which any woman contemplating entrepreneurship should consider carefully.

"I only would choose something I love to do, something I'm happy in," says Klinger. "That's what I advise for everyone. You have to believe in what you are doing. You have to give your best to everyone. The question shouldn't be, 'what can I get out of it?' It should be 'what can I do?'"

Klinger urges her skin care regimen on potential customers with the same heartfelt fervor that Fields offers her bags of warm cookies. She does not give the impression of "making a sale" for the sake of turning a profit so much as out of a genuine desire to help someone else improve their skin. For Fields, the thought of boosting someone's spirits or improving their day, through enjoying her cookies, seems more important than improved profit margins. "You absolutely cannot pursue money as the focal point of your career," Fields says. "Because you will never be happy. If, in fact, you do something that you love, and feel good about it, [then] as you begin to make money, that's the double reward. I run into people who say 'Debbi, I want to make a million dollars. Tell me how to do it.' I can't. Maybe you can [make a million], but I don't know if you'll ever be satisfied."

That said, it should also be noted that none of these women would have stayed in business had it not been financially rewarding. They don't discount the satisfaction they derive from making money as a result of their creative efforts and hard work, and they obviously enjoy the benefits of their labor. They are well aware of the freedom their fortunes afford them because none of these women inherited tremendous wealth. Most have or can afford a household staff, as well as luxuries such as expansive homes or expensive sportscars. Lillian Katz gestures around her striking Manhattan apartment, while having a pedicure, and admits that she lives well. Mary Kay Ash's palatial home is a favorite sightseeing spot for her employees, and Sandra Kurtzig remembers fondly the fun of buying her first Ferrari.

But for Ellen Terry, who was motivated by the cold reality of having to support herself, the fruits of her labor are probably the most sweet. She still savors the moment she walked into an automobile dealership several years ago and purchased a two door Mercedes. Even though her financial advisors didn't recommend having that much money tied up in a car, Terry insisted on paying cash. It wasn't the status of driving a Mercedes again that Terry craved, so much as the symbol of independence, of success, that it represented. Paying cash for the same item that once symbolized the bursting of her velvet bubble, meant more to her than prudent spending. No one, Terry explains, will ever be able to show up on her doorstep and claim her car—or send her world crashing around her—again. By starting her own business, and taking charge of her own destiny, Terry achieved not simply material wealth but a measure of independence that cannot be snatched away. That is reason enough to gamble.

That Incredible, Enviable Confidence

"I could do anything I wanted to do, if I
wanted to do it badly enough, and I was
willing to pay the price."

*W*hen Mary Kay Ash was a child, the telephone
served as an umbilical cord to her mother, a
lifesaving link for a little girl shouldering tremendous responsibility.

"Imagine a seven-year-old who had to stand on a box
to reach the stove, and here she's telling me how to fix
spaghetti or potato soup or whatever. I think she was thinking to herself, 'Oh, what I'm putting on this little kid's
shoulders.'"

Ash's father, ill since her birth, was hospitalized when
she was two years old and did not come home for five years.
When he returned, Ash's mother was working day and night
to provide necessities for the family. Ash, the youngest of
four children by eleven years, was given responsibility for
the household chores.

"I took care of my father, and my mother had a very
hard time just keeping everything paid," Ash says of her
Depression era upbringing. Her mother worked as a restaurant manager, often leaving for work at 5 A.M. and returning

home at 9 P.M. "For many of my early years I was asleep when she left, and asleep when she came home."

Her mother talked to Ash on the phone frequently, offering advice and encouragement as the little girl tried to run the household. "I guess I called her twenty times a day," Ash remembers, "asking, 'How do you do this? How do you do that? How do you make potato soup? or Daddy wants spaghetti for supper, how do you do it?'

"She would tell me in great detail what to do, then she always finished up with, 'Now honey, Mother knows you can do it. You can do it.' I really think she was saying, 'I'm not so sure you can do it.'"

The heavy load of responsibility, and the experience she gained as a result, gave Ash more than a weighty burden to bear at a young age. It also instilled in her the characteristic imperturbable self-confidence and independence found in most successful entrepreneurs. "Mother constantly reinforced my self-image," Ash says. "That I could do anything in this world I wanted to do, if I wanted to do it badly enough, and I was willing to pay the price."

One of the most striking qualities that all of these women possess is that unswerving self-confidence Ash personifies today. It is an intangible quality that permeates everything they do, from the way they carry themselves the moment they walk into a room, to their senses of humor, which may take the form of gentle self-deprecation. Like everyone else, these women have their share of self-doubts in certain areas. Even Debbi Fields, whose youthful beauty turns heads on the street, still worries about her appearance, for instance. But when it comes to believing in their overall ability to get the job done, these women are supremely confident. The confidence they exude, while readily apparent, does not manifest itself in an off-putting cockiness or an egocentric attitude. It is instead confidence at its best, a quiet sense of assurance and security. These women know without a doubt who they are and what they are capable of accomplishing, once they put their minds to it. As a group, they are independent individuals who love being challenged and setting goals—knowing that they can, and will, meet them.

Where does such enviable self-assurance spring from? Most of them credit particularly strong parents, such as Ash's mother, or other influential relatives, for their strong self-images. Experts have theorized that successful male entrepreneurs generally feel close to their mother and disappointed by, or competitive with their fathers. In the cases of these women, that theory doesn't hold true. Generally, they came from traditional, intact families where both parents were influential, or because of circumstances such as the illness of Ash's father, there may have been one influential person present in their lives who imbued them with a strong self-image. Those influential others generally were not "stage mothers" who pushed or prodded them toward any kind of professional success for their vicarious gratification, but simply caring people who encouraged them to do whatever they wanted, as well as they could, whenever possible.

"My parents always instilled in me a strong sense of self-worth," says Ellen Terry. "I've always been an achiever, even when I was a little kid." While growing up, "the underlying message was, you can do anything you want to do."

Cathy Guisewite received that same message. When she was an elementary school student, she brought her childish drawings and stories home and proudly showed them to her parents. Her mother didn't just exclaim over them, pat her daughter on the head, and tack the artwork to the refrigerator, however. "Most mothers say it's nice and they share it with the grandparents," Guisewite says. "Mine sent them to magazines to be published. I had my first rejection letter at age seven."

Guisewite paid no attention to the rejection letters however, because her parents continued to encourage her constantly. "We were told you could do anything," she says, echoing what many other entrepreneurial women say. "'You can go into this business. You could be a great artist if you want. You really have potential as a writer. You have great talent.'"

Guisewite credits her current success as one of the country's leading cartoonists in no small part to her mother's confidence in her. When Guisewite was working as an advertising agency executive, she became frustrated with the imbalance between her professional and personal life. Her career was progressing nicely, Guisewite says, but her love life was "pathetic." One night, she illustrated letters to her parents with small, humorous drawings conveying the frustrations she felt. "Instead of writing about it, I drew a picture of what I looked like, waiting for the phone to ring, eating everything in the refrigerator," she says. "In picture form the pathetic situation looked sort of funny. So I sent it to my parents, to let them know I was coping with humor and creativity."

She kept sending the drawings with her letters home, and her mother, just as she had when Guisewite was a child, again saw publication potential. "Mom thought they were marketable. She thought they were the makings of a comic strip," Guisewite says. "I reminded her of all the things she had submitted in the past, and that this was yet another one—to give up."

Guisewite was perfectly content working in advertising, but her mother kept encouraging her to pursue the possibility of a comic strip. She went to the library and researched comic strip syndicates and which artists they represent, then she typed a list of who her daughter should submit her work to, in the order she felt they should be approached. "Finally, to get her off my back, I sent my work to the name at the top of the list," Guisewite says.

Universal Press Syndicate headed the list, and executives there liked what they saw. Guisewite signed a contract with Universal in 1976 and quickly drew her way into the hearts of millions with her wide-eyed, slightly plump, vulnerable-but-hopeful character, Cathy.

For potential entrepreneurs searching themselves for visible measures of that same positive self-image, the experience of these women shows that outwardly apparent accomplishments aren't necessarily the best gauge. In school for instance, where parents often watch performance anxiously to measure potential success, many of these women were good students, earning "A" averages, but others were average pupils, and some describe themselves as poor performers. All of these women are highly intelligent, but some noted they were not challenged in school or were simply not interested in academics. That example may be the best way of explaining the unusual brand of self-confidence these women possess. Even when they weren't the best or the brightest at everything, *these women invariably came to believe in their ability to achieve success when they wanted to.*

Often their biggest motivation to succeed as children came from a desire to please those influential others who provided constant encouragement. Several of these women describe their adolescent selves as "pleasers," people who tried to make others happy. Although many of them don't see the constant striving to please others as a totally positive adult trait, Debbi Fields says it has helped her business tremendously. When she was growing up she wanted to be a psychiatrist so she could "take care of people." She didn't become a psychiatrist but Fields says she has achieved her goal in a roundabout way. "I selected this business based on an emotional impact it was having for me," she says. "I wanted to make the best cookie. I wanted to make people smile."

Fields serves as an example that it's never too late to change one's self-image. She grew up with a poor self-concept she says, but her parents emphasized the value of hard work and independence to her and her four sisters. "The work ethic in my family was the most important thing," Fields says. "If, in fact, you work hard, you can absolutely pursue your dreams." She later combined that belief with the self-confidence which blossomed with help from husband Randy. Fields married when she was twenty and credits Randy with her improved sense of self. "He kept telling me I was smart, I was capable, I could do it." Even though her husband doubted her business concept at the start, he never doubted her abilities.

Like Fields, Faith Popcorn's strong sense of self-worth didn't come from her mother or father. Because her lawyer parents were often absent, Popcorn's grandparents influenced her significantly, constantly bolstering her confidence and ambition. "I wasn't a good student, I wasn't a good athlete," Popcorn says, "but I knew I could do whatever I wanted. I guess everybody told me."

Her grandparents insisted she had no limitations, Popcorn says. "If I would get in trouble in school, they'd say the teacher was wrong."

Their unconditional confidence in her included a disregard for the rules that bound others, which didn't always prove to be beneficial. "For a long time I thought it was bad because it really made me a different drummer. I didn't have the same rulebook at all," she says. "I guess there was a part of me, like any nonconformist, [that] what I really wanted, more than anything else in the world, was to belong."

Popcorn is not the only entrepreneurial woman to remember feeling a certain distance during childhood. Today these women are all very much in control and more than adept in business and social situations. They are outgoing, friendly, and accustomed now to being in the public eye. But many of them, while saying they were often surrounded by a group of friends, also recall feeling somehow separate from the crowd while growing up.

"I don't remember in school doing group things," says Guisewite. "I had a group of girlfriends, but I'd say I did more things with my family than school things.

"The crowd," she says laughing, "always went off in a different direction and nobody told me where they were going."

Though Guisewite makes that remark jokingly, and those who have a tendency to be loners don't seem bothered by it, Fields remembers numerous hurtful experiences, which even now bring a distressed expression to her face. "I didn't have a lot of friends, and I found that to be very painful," she says. "I tried to do everything in my power to make people like me. It just didn't seem to work."

Many of these women can relate to those feelings, but at the same time they say they wanted to belong, they never wanted to do so at the price of their individuality. Just as Popcorn describes herself as a nonconformist, an equally strong individualistic streak is present in these entrepreneurs. "I don't want to be one of the herd," says Lillian Katz. That sentiment is echoed by Georgette Klinger. "I just wanted to be me in everything," Klinger says. "Maybe I wanted to be the best. I did not want to be a number. I did not want to be a conformer."

Those conflicting feelings, of being disturbed at being left out, but preferring an individual to a group mentality, may account for the appeal that independence and self-sufficiency held for these women early in life. Several of them, for instance, remember their first job fondly—not because of the money they earned, but because of the opportunity it afforded them to be self-sufficient and to excel at the same time.

"I found, when I was sixteen, that if you earned your own thirty-five cents an hour, you didn't have to explain to anybody what you were going to do with it," says Diane Seelye Johnson. For Popcorn, who had not been allowed to work during adolescence, her initial employment experience changed her life. She worked for an advertising agency her first summer in college and liked it so much, she changed her career plans. "I was so intrigued with being at all self-sufficient—they paid me $85 a week—I took this job and didn't go to law school," she says.

Others showed an affinity for independence at an even earlier age. Kay Koplovitz says her first business negotiation came at age four. "My parents were building a new home in the next town. I told my father, it was fine with me if we moved to the next town, but I intended to go to the same kindergarten. I'm sure he looked at me with disbelief, but he asked me how much was the bus fare . . . I had my allowance increased by fifty cents a week to take the bus.

"His best friend said, 'Well, you wanted her to be independent—and she is.'"

Independence and confidence are essential to a woman who runs her own business. And it is a combination that works because its goal is not money, or the chance to prove personal worth by beating someone else, but competing for the sheer joy of it.

Fields remembers her constant efforts to be the best at one of her first jobs. "Even in my little simple jobs I gave 100 percent," she says. "If they expected me to be there, I wanted to be able to say I did this job exquisitely well. When I was fifteen and working at Mervyn's [department store], I made a real issue of making certain my sock tables were perfect. The boys' department belonged to me. I had to put my sign on every day that I worked, and said 'I was here, I'm going to make a difference.' Whether I was being paid minimum wage or not, was not relevant. I wasn't working for money. I was working because I wanted people to know I took pride in what I was doing."

People who know Sandra Kurtzig don't question her competitiveness, but she stresses that it's an inner spirit of competition. "I clearly am competitive, but I'm more competitive with myself," she explains. "I don't go around and say, 'hey look, I'm beating you.'"

That's typical of the nature of competitiveness and confidence expressed by these entrepreneurial women. They are quietly secure about their ability to do the job; and they want to do it to the best of their ability, for the best reason of all: because it enables them to contend with their toughest competition—themselves. *These women don't measure their success in relation to other people, but in relation to themselves.*

The combination of self-confidence, a slight feeling of estrangement, plus a yen for independence, and a healthy dose of competitiveness, might sound like a perfect recipe for breeding entrepreneurism.

There's no such formula however, if the experiences of these women are any indication. Just as potential entrepreneurs may be pleased to note that not all successful entrepreneurs are straight "A" students, neither were they all single-minded, career-oriented children. Most of them consider themselves ambitious people, but few had any specific, much less lofty, goals when growing up. Though it was not a conscious aspiration, most of these women assumed they would become wives and mothers. Generally, those age forty and under, also planned to work outside the home at something, but they felt little sense of professional direction or ambition. For the most part, their plans were vague, their aspirations relatively humble: Ellen Terry wanted to be a teacher; Faith Popcorn wanted to be an actress. Mary Kay Ash wanted to be a nurse; Debbi Fields thought about becoming a psychiatrist. Diane Seelye Johnson considered working as a librarian or an interior decorator, While Paula Stringer wanted to write. Cathy Guisewite dreamed of being a cowboy. And Kay Koplovitz fantasized about working as a cowboy or a ballerina. Others had no particular plans or dreams at all.

But while they didn't have specific, or particularly awesome career aspirations growing up, today these women almost unanimously describe themselves as ambitious. Their ambitions however, are not primarily for more money, plusher offices or bigger titles. *They are ambitious for challenge today, the way they were ambitious for independence as children.*

Georgette Klinger says her skin care salons have grown through the years because of both customer demand and the pleasure she derives from ever expanding challenges, not from burning ambition for more money or fame. "[If] I feel I have to do something else, [it's] not because of what it's going to bring me, but the excitement of it," she says, "of opening another one [salon] and training another one [person], and aggravating myself."

A personal sense of accomplishment is also what keeps Guisewite pushing herself, not a measure of how she stacks up against competitors. "Right now I'd say my main drive is competition against my own potential," Guisewite says.

That personal push often results in descriptions of these women as "driven." Many of them use the word to describe themselves, but they do so cautiously, being sensitive to the negative connotation the word sometimes carries. In reference to men, the term often connotes dedication to excellence, but when used to describe women, it conjures up images of a hard-nosed, obsessive workhorse, an image not many women consider flattering. The drive these women exhibit is not the negative, obsessive definition typically associated with "driven," but a positive, goal-oriented desire to achieve. "I wouldn't say 'driven' . . . " says Popcorn. "I'd say 'focused.'"

"I am ambitious for whatever my next goal is," says Koplovitz. "I don't reach them all. I guess it's not flattering to say that you're ambitious, but I am. It smacks of Lady Macbeth and things like that. [But] I don't think there's anything wrong with ambition. I think ambition is a good thing to have—as long as it's directed in a positive way, and not a negative way."

The ambitions of these women may not have been evident as children, but their tendency to be achievers, their taste for independence, and above all, their absolute confidence in their abilities, often foreshadowed their entrepreneurial futures.

In the final analysis, if there is anything that sets these successful entrepreneurial women apart from the crowd, it is that incredible self-confidence, so often lacking in others.

"Women can always be more confident than their natures let them be," says Guisewite. "I think they're sort of raised up to not be that confident. Women tend to be more insecure from the starting gate than men."

Interestingly, it is her character Cathy's very combination of brimming self-confidence and agonizing insecurity that has endeared her to women around the world. Though women of the '80s are supposed to be self-assured, secure, always in control, they still battle centuries of tradition that dictates women be more self effacing than self confident, more dependent than independent. Societal changes have resulted in more confident, but often more confused women, which "Cathy" personifies uniquely. Women of the '80s identify strongly with the familiar cartoon character and her dilemmas, whether she's handling a delicate professional situation at the office, or debating over which junk food to devour first.

"If Cathy has been anything to women, she has been sort of a relief type of role model," Guisewite says, "Someone who is trying to achieve and trying to make it, but she doesn't give it up entirely if she doesn't. She doesn't end the diet because she eats her lunch on the way to the office in the morning."

Like Guisewite, much of Mary Kay Ash's success has come from her ability to relate to and vanquish the self-doubts of women, for whom confidence seldom comes naturally. Her business strength, Ash says, is motivating people, something anyone who watches her in action knows she can do like few others. During seminars and speeches, she uses catchy phrases, songs, and her own experience to constantly reassure and inspire the thousands of women who work for Mary Kay Cosmetics. She exhorts and encourages them to, above all, be confident in their ability to achieve.

"If you would ask me what is the common denominator among women, I would have to say it's a lack of confidence in their own God given ability," Ash laments. *"They don't believe in themselves."*

For the former little girl who tackled the task of making dinner for her ailing father by standing on a box and listening to her mother's constant encouragement, that quality is paramount to entrepreneurial success.

THREE

The Gender Factor

"I would prefer to be interviewed as an entrepreneur, rather than a 'lady' entrepreneur. I find that should be in the past. For me it is."

*W*hen a potential buyer researches information on ASK Computer Systems Inc. in the business pages of their local newspaper, "It doesn't say next to it, 'F' for female or 'M' for male," founder and chairman Sandra Kurtzig points out. "They buy our stock based on earnings per share and whether or not we're going to grow."

That's why she took ASK public in 1981, Kurtzig says. "That was one of the reasons—to be judged. That's the ultimate report card on equality."

ASK was nine years old when Kurtzig decided to go public. The business that had begun in the spare bedroom of her California apartment, as a way for the young mother to earn a little extra money and keep busy while her children slept, had grown to amazing proportions. Kurtzig's initial $2,000 investment started a company that, by developing and selling computer software to businesses, had earnings of $1.5 million on sales of $13 million by 1981.

Despite the company's impressive track record, Kurtzig wanted to put ASK to the ultimate test: the open market. The necessary paperwork was drawn up, and an elaborate slide show and presentation was prepared to showcase the offering. Kurtzig was preparing to leave for Europe to drum up interest through a whirlwind tour of financial capitals when the company's investment banker pulled her aside.

The conservative financial executive quietly guided Kurtzig to a private office and closed the door for a one-on-one conversation. He repeated what he'd already said several times: "No one has seen a woman CEO of a high-tech company before. You're a novelty. Half of them are going to show up to see the freak show to begin with."

Kurtzig, accustomed by now to this litany, waited for the unknown bombshell her advisor seemed about to drop.

"It's certainly not going to help," he said finally, "to have those long red fingernails." He solemnly advised her to cut them short and paint them a pale color, which she did.

"I was very surprised," Kurtzig remembers. "I was worrying about the profits the next quarter."

Though she tells the story with a laugh, the debate over Kurtzig's fingernail color and length highlights a very real issue. Like it or not—and most successful entrepreneurial women don't—gender is still a factor in the business world, even when the business is your own. The freedom of working for yourself, and not having to answer to anyone else, is often cited by many people as a prime reason to become an entrepreneur, but a great part of the success of entrepreneurism is an ability to deal with others. They must sell not only their product, but themselves as well. Despite the burgeoning female work force, for some businesspeople, dealing with a woman in a professional capacity is still an awkward encounter. These entrepreneurial women have learned how to make colleagues and coworkers feel more at ease, to cope, undisturbed by the gender factor.

Ideally of course, gender would not be an issue. Both

sexes would be considered not alike, but equally competent, an acknowledgment of the different strengths both men and women bring to the businessworld.

"I don't think of myself as a woman or a man," says Kay Koplovitz. "In business situations, I'm just there like they are. I earned my stripes."

"I have a terrible problem with these interviews," says Lillian Katz. "I would prefer to be interviewed as an entrepreneur, rather than a 'lady' entrepreneur. I find that should be in the past. For me it is."

But for others, Katz admits, it is not.

According to government statistics, in 1950, less than 30 percent of the labor force consisted of women; by 1982, women accounted for 43 percent. More importantly, since the 1960s, women have represented the major share of labor force growth, and in the 1980s women are projected to account for seven out of ten additions to the work force.

As more and more women enter the labor market, they have ceased to be a rarity in business, but while the number of women in the labor force as a whole is large, the number of women at the executive level is still appallingly small. Of the Fortune 500 companies, the 500 largest industrial companies in the U.S., only one woman executive, Katharine Graham of *The Washington Post*, made the 1986 list. (She initially inherited the position through family control of the company.) Later that year, another woman, Linda Wachner, did take over a Fortune 500-sized company, an apparel business called Warneco, bringing the number to two.

It may be trendy to pay lip service to the idea of executive women, but despite the ever increasing number of women in business, only 2 percent of the top executive ranks are occupied by women. In absolute numbers, that translates to twenty-nine women out of 1,362 respondents, according to the Korn/Ferry study.

In short, the board room is still overwhelmingly dominated by three-piece, pinstriped suits, locker room camaraderie, and an effective good old boy system. For many women the board room remains an exclusive club, one they probably won't be invited to join. The outlook for future female executives is not particularly encouraging either. Though a decade ago less than 10 percent of business graduate school degrees were awarded to women, and today's classes boast an enrollment of approximately 30 percent women, there are indications that despite the increased presence of more qualified women, they aren't necessarily taking significant posts in the corporate world. Those women of a decade ago have not climbed the corporate career ladder as successfully as their male counterparts, and in some cases are jumping off the ladder completely. While it is true that the first class of women MBAs graduated in 1976, and are just now reaching their mid-thirties, and the Korn/Ferry profile says today's typical senior executive is fifty-one years old, a survey conducted by *Fortune* magazine reveals a surprising trend. According to the survey of MBA graduates from the class of 1976, 30 percent of 1,039 women were self-employed or unemployed. But only 21 percent of the 4,255 men surveyed were in the same circumstances.

The feminine trend away from the corporate climb is attributable to several factors.

Some women leave the corporate world because they grow impatient with the lengthy climb it takes to get to the top of an established entity, and/or their inability to break the "glass ceiling." Some are leaving not only the corporate world, but dropping out of the work force completely, in favor of staying home and raising their children, finding the struggle of being both a professional and a parent more than they want to handle. The harsh reality of the effort it takes to succeed in the business world and juggle domestic responsibilities simultaneously has left some women disillusioned. "Right now it's a fight," says Mary Kay Ash. "And I think that's why they're going home. It's a tough, every-minute-of-the-day fight." Still others are choosing to start businesses at home in an effort to have at least part of both worlds.

The sparsity of women in the established corporate executive suite comes as no surprise to Faith Popcorn, "It's no accident that there's no Fortune 500 company other than Kay Graham, with a female chairman," notes Popcorn. "People say, 'Well the business people [women] haven't come up yet.' That's not true. In the early '70s they all graduated and we're still waiting. It's not happening. Somebody had to be good enough."

Popcorn, whose reputation for predicting trends based on cultural currents is well known, says she foresaw the present trend toward women bailing out of the corporate work force several years ago.

The businesswomen of the '70s were good enough to climb the corporate ladder, Popcorn theorizes, but today "nobody wants them," particularly the executive men who have dominated the business world for centuries.

"Why should they?" she asks. "People that usually have the power base don't hand it over to be nice. They're comfortable with other men. It's much more comfortable to stay the way they are than to change."

The business world, Popcorn adds, didn't really need women. "It seemed to be rolling along," she says, smiling. But women decided they were tired of being relegated to low quality jobs, and "they weren't going to put up with it anymore. So then they said, 'I can do this.' Of course they can . . . I think men would have been much smarter to make women more proud and equal of their home jobs."

Whether men could have averted the trend to women working outside the home or not is, of course, a moot point. Women have obviously joined the work force for good, and men must accept and adjust to them as equals in the business world. Change in that direction is occurring, but the pace is sometimes agonizingly slow. According to *Inside Corporate America* by Allan Cox, 85 percent of top executives say their companies are eager to promote women to middle management positions, but only 68 percent support moving women into top executive spots. Many men it seems, are willing to work *with* women, but are less than thrilled at the idea of working *for* them. According to the Heidrick & Struggles survey, that continuing discomfort of management with women in executive positions is considered to be the primary reason women go into business for themselves.

Louise Vigoda, who deals with men more often than women in her business as a real estate developer, agrees that the historically empowered are not particularly eager to turn their power base over to newcomers. "Men had a damn good thing going," she notes. "Why should they [want to deal with women] more than they want any other immigrants? Why should they? They've got to deal with competition for their jobs. They've got to deal with strange creatures. They didn't grow up in the locker room with them."

The chilly reception given businesswomen has not been quick to thaw, and the blame lies partially with women themselves. The responsibility for some men's inability to relate to women as executive equals, is laid at least in part at the feet of early businesswomen.

When women first began entering the work force en masse, they didn't always make it easy for members of the opposite sex. The "first generation" of businesswomen made one critical mistake many women are still paying for: *they tried to make their gender a non-issue by minimizing the differences between the sexes and adopting the attitudes of the majority.* Instead of emphasizing the strengths of the feminine sex, such as sensitivity, intuition, and even the femininity which set them apart from the male crowd, they appeared to be not only businesslike, but masculine. Men can accept women who conduct themselves as professionals, theorize some business veterans, but they are at a loss how to work with a woman who looks and acts like a man.

"Men, when you go into a board room with them . . . they absolutely want you to be businesslike, but they want you to be a lady," says Ellen Terry. "They don't want you to take on the characteristics of a man. I think many times women try to act like a man in their approach. I don't think you have to do that. I think you can be tough minded and also soft and feminine at the same time."

"Men know how to deal with women as women," explains Kurtzig. "They know how to deal with their sisters who are women, they know how to deal with their daughters who are women. They know how to deal with their wives who are women, and they know how to deal with the fact that women get pregnant, that women are different . . . If you act like a woman I think men know how to deal with you. Then the equality doesn't become as much of an issue, as if you're up there trying to act as something they don't understand."

Randy Fields, husband of Debbi Fields, agrees.

"The first generation of women that went into business decided to play by men's rules instead of women's rules, which I think was a tragic mistake," Fields says. "If I was going to negotiate with Arnold Palmer, I wouldn't do it on the golf course with golf clubs. I'd rather do it from my own turf, where my strengths are. Women went into business with suits and the MBAs in financial analysis and tried to play in a man's world. They didn't play their strong hand."

Unfortunately the first generation of businesswomen had no "home turf" from which to negotiate, no tradition to refer to, and little formal business background on which to draw. As newcomers to the business world they found themselves playing a new game on an unfamiliar field, with all the disadvantages that includes.

In hindsight, Fields' point is well made: women should have worked harder at carving out their own turf, their own methods of doing business, thereby accentuating their strengths, rather than trying to use the techniques and tactics invented by men for men.

The entrepreneurial women who call their own shots don't make that mistake. These women *capitalize* on their femininity. When it comes to their wardrobes for instance, the majority of entrepreneurial women interviewed take special pains to look attractive, to accent, not downplay, their femininity. None of them confuse "sexiness" with "femininity," so that you don't see them wearing plunging necklines or see-through blouses, but you do see these women wearing fashionable, colorful business attire, right down to their silk blouses and high heels.

You will not find them clad in the "dress for success" pinstriped navy skirt and jacket, with the no-nonsense bow blouse and sensible shoes. According to the Heidrick & Struggles survey, only 18.9 percent of female corporate executives agreed with that approach, and it is a uniform that causes entrepreneurial women to wince and groan.

"If I dislike anything, it's a woman with her ties and bows and blouses," says skin care expert Georgette Klinger, who wears soft feminine looks. Because of Klinger's vested interest in beauty, her dislike of the "power suit" might be expected. But Popcorn and others who have no commercial interest in the beauty business, are equally as disdainful of the "dress for success" uniform. "I don't dress that way," Popcorn says, "middle managers dress that way."

Debbi Fields is just as wary of the power dressing formula, which she dubs a concept dangerous to the future of women in business. "I am very interested in making certain that I don't fall into a stereotype," she says. "I really believe people have to be comfortable. I dress according to how I feel comfortable."

She purposely avoids the skirted business suit, in favor of silk dresses or other more feminine attire, because of the cold, austere image a suit connotes. "I really believe in being feminine," Fields says. "Sometimes people will assume if you're going to be a woman in business' that you're going to have to live in a man's world. That's stereotyped. That's conservative. It's a bow tie."

And it's not only unnecessary, it's not advisable, Fields adds. "Women are coming into their own, saying 'I am very bright, I'm extremely capable, I'm going to dress the way I want to dress. That does not take away anything in terms of the job that they do." For many of these successful entre-preneurial women their clothes are simply that, an exten-sion of their self-confidence. *They are not concerned with dressing to convey an image to others; they are interested in dressing to feel good about themselves, which includes being both professional and feminine.* That marks a tremendous change in attitude: because they are sure of their abilities, these women don't have any insecurities to mask or any false fronts of bravado to erect. They don't feel the need to camouflage the fact that they are indeed women, and they feel comfortable wearing simple silk dresses or outfits that don't shout "power" messages. They are confident they al-ready possess power—at no loss to their femininity.

Cartoonist Cathy Guisewite also dislikes and eschews the "power suit" but she is not so quick to dismiss its past usefulness. The severe, conservative look served a purpose once she points out. Women who entered the business-world, before they became commonplace there, needed a uniform of sorts as an attention getting device to emphasize their presence. It took a "radical departure from the cute little gingham dresses in the office, to a stern, serious busi-ness suit for women to be taken seriously," she says.

However the idea was carried to an extreme, Guisewite agrees. The neuter suit look was "not acknowledging that there are some qualities of being feminine versus being masculine that were good for the corporation, that make a better team. I think it was a mistake, for everybody, for people to think that women had to turn into men."

Just as their appearance may be subject to misinterpretation at times, so are their actions and attitudes, say some entrepreneurial women. Regretably, old jokes often ring truer than they would like, for example, that men who go after what they want are called "aggressive," while women who display the same characteristic often are considered "obnoxious." Men who attain a certain level of achievement and wealth are called "powerful;" women at the same level often are perceived as "intimidating." That may be especially true when the CEO is not just a highly paid executive, but the founder and creative genius behind the company.

Popcorn wants to be perceived the way she sees herself: as aggressive, but not obnoxious. It disturbs her that some people consider her intimidating. "Everybody wants to be liked," she notes wryly. "Dale Carnegie explained that." On occasion, when she realizes she is coming across too forcefully during a meeting or discussion, she consciously slows down and pulls back. "It's like this rush of power," she says. "When I really want to get something done, it's almost physical. I almost see people jump back. I really have to moderate it and say, 'Faith, go a little slower.'"

Like Popcorn, Louise Vigoda takes special pains to moderate any perceptions of herself as intimidating. She too finds such ideas troublesome. "I'm five-feet-nine-and-a-half [inches tall]," she notes, "and if I have a little short man come in, I'll never stand up when he comes through that door."

In all fairness, as Popcorn points out, people often find successful men equally intimidating. But the intimidation factor is more acute and problematic among women. "We're not used to perceiving women as successful," Popcorn says. "It's very new to our culture, and we're not sure we like it very much. I think we all feel like we're losing our mothers."

Women are not losing the qualities traditionally associated with motherhood, but the role is changing and expanding. Businesswomen, both those who are actually somebody's mother and those who are not, leave behind the soft, emotional side of themselves, associated with "mothering" when they go to the office. Unfortunately, in trying to leave that role at home many women try too hard and come across as cold and unfeeling. Women who do that are just as much of a problem for businesswomen trying to strike a balance between femininity and professionalism, as the one who brings the mother role to the office with her.

"I think in a way women who are competitive are seen to be bitches," says Kurtzig, who describes herself as aggressive but not cutthroat. "Women have to be competitive in a different way in order to be successful. I think they're trying so hard to assert themselves, to say they're a woman and they can be equal, and they're going to do it, that it comes across as very hard, rather than competitive. I think this is a big problem with a lot of women."

Most of these women are so successful, that asserting themselves isn't a problem. If anything, they concentrate on softening their approach, rather than on toughening up to do battle in the business world. They want to be respected, not feared.

When Mary Kay Ash walks into a room full of men, she makes a point of looking as pretty as possible and acting as feminine as possible. Using her appearance as a distraction, she says she keeps her mouth shut, "until I really know what I'm talking about, so that they have to guess whether I'm being extremely brilliant or dumb."

Ash is not the only woman who has learned how to turn her sex into an advantage. Most successful entrepreneurial women learn early on to not only cope with their gender and the added dimensions it brings to the business-world, but to use it to their benefit. *That doesn't mean batting the eyelashes and employing feminine wiles. It does mean pressing an advantage, including the element of surprise, just as any shrewd businessman would.*

Sandra Kurtzig says being different can be helpful. For one thing, it immediately makes you more noticeable.

"If you're selling a product against five men, who probably have equally good products, and you're probably selling it to a man, you want anything you can have that's going to make you unique, or stand out, or be remembered or have your product remembered," Kurtzig says. "The fact that you're a woman selling against five men with equally good products, the prospect will probably remember you."

Clients and colleagues aren't the only ones who will remember you, as these women well know. So will members of the media.

The news spotlight is often easier to garner for women. When women achieve even a small measure of business success it is often overexposed, simply because they are different. It's easier to attract the attention of the press being a woman in a predominantly male field, because the novelty appeals to journalists hungry for stories about "breakthroughs" and "firsts." "When you're the only woman doing something you get more attention, simply because you are a woman, whether you deserve it or not," says Kay Koplovitz. "You're more likely to get positive press. When you do something wrong you may be more likely to get negative press as well, but I think you get opportunities. You get asked to speak and you're given platforms to say things because you are the first."

Cathy Guisewite says being a woman in the comic strip business helped her because the time was ripe for a legitimate expression from a woman in the field. But in addition, "I think I have gotten proportionately more attention for my strip because I'm a woman," Guisewite says. "I've gotten a lot more publicity. I think things have been promoted a little bit harder, because I'm unique as a woman doing this."

Though women business owners are obviously more noticeable in a male dominated field, many women say their male coworkers don't seem particularly concerned by their presence. Many men unwittingly give women colleagues an advantage by failing to treat them like competition. Instead, they note, men often were surprisingly helpful on the way up, partially because they don't feel the same keen sense of competition with women that they do with other men. Kurtzig jokes that being a woman helped her get ASK started because "men always felt like they had to pay for lunch. It helped expenses." Most men are brought up that way, to pick up the check, to open doors, pull out chairs, carry heavy items, and generally be helpful to the feminine sex. That tendency becomes second nature to them and they may extend it unthinkingly to the business arena. Aiding another man on the other hand, a traditional rival, goes directly against such traditional upbringing, and chances are they would rarely make that mistake. That urge to be helpful to women occasionally blinds male executives to legitimate competition from females, offering women the advantageous element of surprise.

"Men don't think women are a real threat," says Kurtzig. "They're 'inferior.' They can't succeed. They think you're cute and harmless. They don't have to pat you on the head, but deep down they don't see you as real competition. Their real competition is that other male. So men are apt to help you more because, if you're successful, that doesn't take away from their ego."

Not only do some men not recognize women as competition, they often don't take them seriously at all. Some men, usually those who still think of women as strictly wives and mothers, also make the mistake of assuming the woman behind the business is merely a figurehead, a front for the company being run by her husband. Though Diane Seelye Johnson and her husband started Central Pipe & Supply together, people often assumed her role was as an employee of her spouse. After ten years in business they no longer ask how she likes working for her husband, Johnson notes, but neither do they ever assume the business is hers. Debbi Fields says she no longer expends energy trying to pierce the myth that the company that grew from one store in 1977 to 350 ten years later, and a multi-million dollar volume, was anybody's brainchild but her own. Even company advisors, who know Debbi is the president in action as well as title, sometimes fail to take her seriously. "To this day I have $3 million in life insurance, and she has $250,000," points out Randy Fields.

Many men realize these women run successful businesses, but they often adopt the attitude, particularly if the woman is married, that the business is merely a hobby, and any financial matter is of only passing interest to a woman. Once again the traditional upbringing that pegs men as breadwinners, and women as helpmates, hampers the ability of men to relate to businesswomen. Often the misperception is unintentional, and men are mystified at women's annoyance over it, but no matter how well intended, the attitude still poses problems to women in business for themselves.

When Johnson and her husband both separately purchased stock in a company as an investment several years ago, she was irritated to find he received notices of annual meetings, but she didn't. When she complained to the man in charge he suggested that her notices must have gotten lost in the mail. She insisted they hadn't, until he finally admitted it was assumed she would share her husband's mail, and she had not been sent the material. His wife, he added pointedly, loved the pedestal she was on.

"Well," replied an annoyed Johnson, "the only things that I ever see on pedestals are inanimate objects—and half of them are covered with bird droppings."

Vigoda has also noticed the tendency of male business colleagues to take her less than seriously. She went into business in the '60s, when women were still rare in the corporate world. "Men really thought it was cute," she says. "That was my sense of it. They thought it was cute or sociologically hip. It was an attitude more than anything. Very few people are gauche enough to say 'You're cute.'"

Once a successful real estate agent did drop by Vigoda's office to talk about her venture into business. "He happened to be on his fourth wife," Vigoda says. "He wanted to talk to me about what I was doing because he thought it was 'really neat' and his present wife 'needs something to do.' I can't tell you how offended I was. It was like he was going to buy her a knitting machine or give her a week at the Golden Door. I didn't know how to answer that."

Even those close to these women, not just colleagues, are occasionally guilty of failing to take their plans seriously. When Johnson announced that she was bored after years as a housewife, her husband suggested she go bowling with friends. When she said she planned to go back to school, he applauded the idea—of taking a course or two. Randy Fields admits that while he encouraged Debbi, he didn't really expect her cookie business to succeed—and neither did their banker who extended the loan. "He even said to Randy, 'This will be a great experience for Debbi, from a 'learning perspective,'" Debbi remembers.

Thankfully, there are some signs, however slow or slight, that gender is becoming less of a factor in the businessworld. The attitudes of men change, with age and experience. "If the man you are talking to is forty-five or over, then he adopts the attitude of, 'Oh hi, you sweet little thing,'" notes Ash. "'Honey, darling, sweetheart.' Kind of a condescending attitude toward women. Now fortunately, the younger men are being brought up with women sitting beside them in school . . . If you're talking to a younger man, under forty-five, as a general rule he will have a much better idea, respect for women, than his [older] counterpart."

Louise Vigoda's experience has been somewhat different. Whether due to the fact that top spots are held by older men or because business veterans are more experienced, Vigoda says, while she was often underestimated and not considered a threat in the beginning, many older men take her seriously as she rises in the business world. "The higher you go, the harder it is, because you are no longer 'cute.' You really are a direct threat," Vigoda notes.

"It is very difficult to be sitting across the table from someone, who probably will not make in a lifetime of salaried employment as much as you make in a year or two, look at you and not resent it," Vigoda says. "There's still the henpecking order. They've grown up with men and they expect there will always be some man who's a top dog. They don't expect it of women. When they see a woman sitting across the table from them, there is a lot of power playing that goes on. They may not make as much money as you, they may not be as successful as you, but they are going to try to show you that they are better than you are. It's the henpecking order. It used to be more crudely expressed in 'Thank God I'm a white man.' It means that no matter what a jerk you are, what an idiot you are, you're better. . . ."

Vigoda and other successful entrepreneurial women long for the day when gender will not be a factor, when their male colleagues won't feel threatened or feel the need to be condescending. They look forward to the time they won't attract attention because they are a minority, when they won't be identified as the "first this," or "the only that." They hope eventually no one will sit up and take notice because of their presence in the board room, preferably because they will have feminine company. When the gender factor no longer exists, perhaps no one will notice the color of their fingernails.

Kurtzig says one of the nicest comments ever made about her, came when a company vice-president was asked what it was like to work for a woman, and he replied that he'd forgotten he worked for one. "That's the highest compliment that you can be paid—when it's not an issue," she says.

Kurtzig considers herself "to be a businessperson who just happens to be a woman. If I were to summarize anything that I hope people see me represent, it's that."

But for the time being, she and others realize the day of gender blindness, when sex is not a factor, is far distant. They are however, encouraged by the small signs that show changes are taking place. For example, when a second public offering for ASK Computer Systems Inc. was made, the company's investment banker pulled Kurtzig aside for another chat. Once again her nails were long and noticeably red.

"I realized, after we went public, that whatever I did to grow the company is what people should be interested in, not the facade," Kurtzig says. "The minute that the [first] offering was done I let my nails grow again, and painted them red again, because that's me."

This time her financial advisor noted that ASK had performed strongly and been well received during the period when Kurtzig's fingernails were long and red.

"Your nails," he told her pointedly, "are not long enough or red enough."

"This time," Kurtzig relates with relish, "he said, 'Don't change anything.'"

FOUR

Feminism and Femininity

"If you're a woman in business and you think you have to choose, I'm saying you don't."

*F*or almost fifteen years, Louise Vigoda was the traditional, ideal wife and mother. Happily married to a successful physician, and the mother of three, she did everything from keeping supper in the warming oven for her husband when he worked late, (and waiting to eat until he came home), to shining his shoes and packing his luggage for him. She drove the carpool to and from the children's activities; she worked as a volunteer for worthy causes; and she made sure the lawn was mowed.

When her youngest child entered first grade, Vigoda started her real estate management and development firm—and kept striving to live up to the traditional ideals of wife and mother, putting in full days at the office and equally full days at home. Finally, she called a halt to the madness.

"I returned home at 7 o'clock one evening, and there at the top of the steps were all the shining faces, my husband and three children, and as I am climbing the stairs, they said, 'What's for dinner?' I said, 'I don't know what's for dinner. Go out and get it.'"

The incident may sound harsh to some when Vigoda relates it, but she uses it to emphasize her change in attitude.

Though her husband was always easygoing and undemanding, for years it didn't occur to her to quit trying to "do it all." In the early days of her business, she took a tiny office and worked part time. "I never left the house until my children had gone to school," she says, "and I was always home when they got back from school. If one of my kids got their finger caught in the Ping-Pong table, or the principal called, or any of those things, I closed the office." But as her business responsibilities increased and her family still clamored for her time, the pressure became unbearable. While trudging up the stairs that evening, she came to a realization: "You start ordering your priorities. Suddenly you realize it really isn't that important. [For example] It's important to eat, but it's not important to eat a particular thing, on a particular date, prepared by a particular person."

Reordering priorities sounds easy in theory, but can be exceedingly difficult in practice, as Vigoda discovered. Though she knew logically that adjustments needed to be made in her work and home duties, common sense didn't automatically assuage the guilt she experienced or the sense of sacrifice she felt for not living up to society's ideal of the perfect wife and mother. The attitudinal and practical changes that followed were as much on her part as they were on her family's. It was not simply a matter of saying no, or explaining calmly why her new professional duties made it impossible for her to continue to fulfill her wife-and-mother roles the way she had in the past. It wasn't just her family, but Vigoda herself who needed to realize that she couldn't "do it all," that she couldn't live up to the Superwoman myth of perfect wife, mother, and consummate career woman.

Vigoda was brought up to follow the traditional path, where the wife serves as the husband's helpmate and support system, assuming primary responsibility for the home and family. When Vigoda took on business responsibilities as well, at age thirty-eight, long after the traditional pat-

·HE RONALD J. DARBY LIBRARY
Northampton High School

terns in their marriage had been established, the change from the original game plan was difficult to orchestrate.

"I would work until he finished his training," Vigoda says of the unspoken outline for her and her physician husband's life. "He would build his practice, we would have three children, and I would sit by the swimming pool, and I would entertain beautifully. Those were the days when women were all things to all people."

What Vigoda terms the "overlap period"—when women were encouraged to work outside the home and maintain their workload at home—has created enormous problems she says. "It's very hard to give up your traditional ideas of your obligations as a good wife," she notes. "But when you pile on to that a full-time career, you are asking for a load that no one should carry."

No one *should* carry it perhaps, but many women do. Despite the unprecedented progress women have made in their professional lives, many have not made equal strides in their personal lives. Women are often expected to shoulder the same responsibilities at home that they did previously, when they didn't work outside the home. Whether that expectation comes from themselves or from others, the burden of trying to live up to it can be overwhelming.

The changes which occurred primarily as a result of the feminist movement did not always free women to have greater choices, but often saddled them with excessive guilt. The pervasive myth of the Superwoman who can have everything easily—job, marriage and family—often raised not only unrealistic expectations, but also created an accompanying sense of guilt that occurs when they can't live up to those expectations. Instead of being given the choice of working at home as mothers, *or* working outside the home as career women, they were given the option of *adding* extra work to their family responsibilities, under the guise of "having it all." Many women believed the dream of "having it all"—the roles of wife, mother, and professional—would somehow be no more difficult than having part of it, and they trotted off to the business world blissfully expectant. For some, a rude awakening came when they discovered the price to be paid.

"I think a lot of women found it to be much harder and a lot less rewarding than they were promised," says Cathy Guisewite. "The promises were very grandiose. You could do anything. You could be president of the company. Nobody mentioned the sacrifices that you have to make and I think many women, to succeed in business, have to sacrifice something in their relationships, more than a man does who succeeds in business."

The difference between promises of how life should be, and the reality of how it is, may be one of the primary reasons that most of these women do not identify strongly with the feminist movement. Women today are less interested in advocating women's rights or feminism than in redefining femininity in general thought, expanding it to include both shrewd business practices and the softer side of womanhood. Despite the fact that some of these women have experienced sexual discrimination, both blatant and subtle, few of these women want to be linked with the women's liberation movement or the organizations that promulgate it.

When Paula Stringer, wife and mother, opened her first real estate office in 1958, she went into business with an unmarried woman. The reason she took on a partner, Stringer says, was because, as an unattached female, a "femme sole," her partner could sign papers. Stringer, a married woman, could not.

After three years, Stringer was ready to open an office of her own, and approached her family banker for a $500 loan. The banker told her he'd be happy to give her the money—as long as her husband's signature appeared on the papers.

"I couldn't run a business that way," says Stringer, still appalled at the idea. So she and her husband went to court, and swore under oath that Stringer would be solely responsible for her own acts.

Despite that experience, Stringer is hesitant to label herself an advocate of women's liberation. "Yes and no," she says when asked if she is a feminist. "I'm still from the old school. I want to be treated like a lady, but I want to have equal rights."

Ambivalence about the organized movement and a simple lack of interest is typical of these entrepreneurial women, not just of those from the "old school," but also from those women age forty and under. They are interested in equal rights as people, not as a special interest group. They want to retain their femininity and be equal, a different-but-equal philosophy that should, ideally, not even be an issue at all. For these women "liberation" is just that, a non-issue.

Many of the older entrepreneurial women encountered obstacles on the road to success, and the younger entrepreneurial women are aware that their way has been smoother because of those obstacles surmounted and eliminated by their predecessors. But despite that awareness and their unequivocal support for equal rights, these women generally have not embraced the feminist movement.

That the women's liberation movement is currently out of favor and is experiencing a negative backlash is obvious when talking to these supremely successful women. They have made a different type of business history from their counterparts who have climbed the corporate ladder, because not only did they reach the executive suite, but through their hard work and determination, they built the company behind that suite. The corporate woman has had her own battles to fight, but financing for instance is not one of them. Financing is still difficult for women to obtain, as shown by the fact that when women start businesses, they still tend to use individual savings as their major source of funding, with joint savings of husbands and wives ranking second. (That may also explain, at least in part, why so many women start businesses on a small basis.)

But despite such difficulties encountered by entrepreneurial women, and despite the irony that their names are often invoked as examples of the "epitome of feminism," the very term "feminist" brings a bored look, or a grimace of distaste to most of them.

Sandra Kurtzig pulls out a dictionary to explain why the term "feminist" has a negative connotation to her. She agrees with the first definition, of "political, economic and social equality of the sexes," Kurtzig says, but takes issue with the second half which reads, "organized activity on behalf of women's rights and interests."

"That's the thing that I find offensive," she says. "I think women don't need to wave a banner of equality. I think if they're really equal, and they're comfortable with the fact that they're equal, they don't need to go waving the banner. They need to just go, and perform, and be themselves. I think the waving of the banner is the problem that men have with women."

Others share Kurtzig's dislike of the militant attitude conveyed by the women's liberation movement. "I believe in women working," says Georgette Klinger, "but I'm not a typical feminist. I believe we had to come through that revolution, evolution. I believe in what they do, but the way they did it, I don't believe in."

Many of these women voiced concern that the militant methods used in decades past may have brought progress at the cost of femininity.

"I was never a part of it, because they stood for a lot of things I don't believe in," says Mary Kay Ash. "They were putting on low heeled shoes, and cutting their hair like men, and taking off their makeup, and burning their bras, and all that business in the early '60s. I think God intended for us to be feminine and women and we should stay that way."

Ash is vocal about the equal rights issue however, and points out that she started her company from a desire to give women an equal opportunity in business. Her refusal to embrace the organized women's liberation movement, like the refusal of others, may spring from the individualistic streak that marks many of these entrepreneurial women. Perhaps the reason they didn't join the movement is simply that entrepreneurs are typically more comfortable acting as individuals than as a group. They are more interested in doing, in taking action where they see a need, than in talking or analyzing the whys and wherefores of that need. They point proudly to what their companies have done for women, despite their personal lack of involvement in the movement.

For Lillian Katz, the problems addressed by the feminist movement are not as important as the actions needed to solve those problems. "I've never worked for NOW," Katz says. "People think I should have worked for NOW. What I did was much better than NOW. I gave women an opportunity to come in to the work force, to come in there and earn $10,000. To earn six figures now, and take that maternity leave, and have all the privileges of motherhood, with all the privileges of career. If NOW can do that, I'd like to know how."

The opposition of older women, those raised with traditional values often at odds with the goals of the feminist movement, might be understandable; but the attitude expressed by these women age forty and under is surprising, especially considering their exposure to the feminist movement during its "glory days."

"I am very grateful for people like Gloria Steinem and Betty Friedan," Kay Koplovitz says, but she notes that the feminist movement never particularly interested her. "I didn't feel an enormous amount of sympathy toward it, nor did I reject it. I thought there was a lot of truth in what they say, but I did not necessarily agree with their methods. I'm grateful there were people on the front lines for me, and that I came behind those people. I am grateful for what they did."

The attitude of indifference on the part of younger women has been referred to as "entitlement" by author Betty Friedan because many of these "second generation" businesswomen, those who followed on the heels of the groundbreakers, don't feel as if equal rights are an issue they have to fight for; it is something they are naturally entitled to. They take equal rights and opportunities for granted. That may represent substantial progress to some, but others see what might be called the "yes but" syndrome—("yes I believe in equal rights, but no I'm not a feminist,")—as a dangerous attitude.

It disturbs Diane Seelye Johnson, for one. The feminist movement finally gave voice to the frustrations she had felt but been unable to express for years. Johnson remembers having to lie about her plans as the spouse of a serviceman in order to get a job, and having to hide her pregnancy later in order to keep a job. She also didn't like reading about legal scholars who classified women "with idiots, infantiles, and senile people in the law," Johnson says. "I didn't like the fact that people expected me to ask my husband's permission to do things. I didn't like the fact that I had lived and been a regular church member, and we went out and raised all this money because our [church] balcony needed carpeting, but the women weren't allowed to choose. We couldn't buy what we'd raised money for, because women were not allowed to make decisions in that church.

"These things sound petty when you start listing them," she says, but, "what worries me about younger women today is you don't know why we're mad and radical."

She is glad that younger women don't understand, because it means they haven't had to go through those experiences, but nonetheless she worries about the future of upcoming generations of women because of it.

The movement's failure to appeal to these successful entrepreneurial women, and to women of the '80s in general, may arise from its failure to address the key issue of motherhood, theorizes Cathy Guisewite who considers herself a feminist. "The definition of feminism is believing in women as of equal human status with men." Guisewite says. "What's not to believe in that? What I've found out about it recently is the biggest problem the feminist movement suffered is never addressing the needs of women to be mothers, never getting political on the issues like child care and maternity, only taking more of a stern, hostile view originally, 'We don't even need men in our lives.' Then, 'Certain liberated men are okay.' But no acknowledgement of women, and their desires to be mothers, and the real practical problems of working that out. I think feminism's future is partly in that, and I think there needs to be sort of a rebirth and a reeducation, so these successful women aren't defensive about being possibly considered a feminist. I think that's awful."

The need to be not just mothers, but businesswomen and mothers, is indeed one of the prime concerns of these women. Studies bear out Guisewite's theory that female executives make more personal sacrifices than men, and that the sacrifices are considerable. The Korn/Ferry executive profile reports that 94 percent of male executives are married, and 95 percent have children. A study on corporate women conducted by the executive search firm, Heidrick & Struggles shows however that almost 20 percent of female executives have never married at all, and the majority of senior executive women have no children.

For those women, "having it all" is not a possibility. Faith Popcorn blames journalist and author Helen Gurley Brown for perpetuating the myth of "having it all" and making it believable. "Helen Gurley Brown did it to us," Popcorn says. "I told her that. I said, 'You did this to us. You told us we could have it all and nobody has.' It takes two days for every one. To really be a good parent and wife takes full time. To be a good businesswoman takes more than full time. So you're cutting down something."

"I don't think there's enough time in the day to have it all at once," agrees Mary Kay Ash. "How can you be a mother to three children, have those cares and worries of a large corporation, and a husband, and all the other things at once? I don't think you can."

Many women, like Louise Vigoda, have tried, going through periods of refusing to cut back their responsibilities in any area—and paying a heavy price in stress and strain. Most of them have come to the conclusion that you can indeed have it all, but not all at once. Sometimes work may suffer, other times family may take a backseat. No one knows that better than entrepreneurial women. For these women the pull between family and career is probably stronger than for corporate career women, because the company is their own. The corporate woman may do so reluctantly, but if absolutely necessary, she can walk away knowing she shares a modicum of responsibility with others. But for entrepreneurial women, ultimate responsibility for the company lies with them, as does responsibility for the family. The trick to balancing the two they say, is prioritizing, managing time efficiently, and for now, learning to live with the guilt most working mothers feel.

"That is a tremendous problem," says Kurtzig, remembering how she felt torn between her business and her family, especially when someone would ask how she could leave town on business when her child had the chicken pox.

Debbi Fields has also felt that familiar agony of being pulled in two directions. "I think every mother that works feels guilty," Fields says. "That's just a personal opinion. Are we spending enough time with our children, and will we regret this in the future?" The moment Fields arrives home from the office at night, her time belongs to the children she says. She makes a point of taking breaks from the business day to attend special events involving her daughters, such as piano recitals or plays. If she feels she hasn't spent enough time with them, she schedules them into her business appointment calendar, and they meet her at the office for lunch.

To these successful entrepreneurs, making such adjustments is simply part of being a businesswoman. There is no secret formula for maintaining the balance. "Women have a harder time juggling it all," Kurtzig says, "because it is *harder* juggling it all."

The guilt that arises from leaving home and children for the office and work appears to be a natural one, a feeling conferred automatically by the biological process of giving birth. It is an emotion even the most caring, concerned, interested father does not experience.

"It doesn't mean I'm a women's libber or a feminist, but I think it's reality that men are not, in the near future, going to be bearing children," says Kurtzig, laughing. "Until that happens there's going to be a difference . . . Women are still going to be the [responsible] ones. Even though my husband shared his responsibilities, when push comes to shove, it was still my responsibility to worry about the children. Maybe I did just take it on naturally. It never became a major issue, but I think women do have this feeling. I don't think he had a guilt feeling for going to work and not staying at home."

The tendency to place children first is natural, agrees Lillian Katz. "She [mother] will fit her business life around those responsibilities. I don't think you can say that about a man," Katz says, pointing out that when her son went into the hospital to have his tonsils taken out, she moved into the room with him during his stay, which even a model father would rarely consider doing.

"A man who has a wife at home, even a working wife, he's always going to get to the office, no matter what," Katz says. "Who stays home when the kids get sick? The mother. And they both have important jobs. I think being a mother you just *do* those things."

Some of these women say there is definitely a choice to be made, and if necessary, there is little question what comes first. "I would give up my career in a minute, before I'd give up my children," says Vigoda.

Georgette Klinger says she doesn't understand women who put career before family. She knew her business suffered while her daughter, Kathryn, was growing up, because she wasn't at the salon from opening to closing as she had been previously. But she says simply, and without apparent conflict, "My first priority was Kathryn."

If forced to choose between home and career, Ellen Terry says she'd take her children without question. But, she adds—and it is an important "but"—she doesn't feel she has to choose. Younger women, those age forty and under, who became businesswomen and wives when traditional female roles were in the throes of tremendous upheaval, are, like Terry, far less willing to accept the notion of being forced to choose one part of their lives over another. Though successful businessmen may wrestle with how much time to spend with their families and their careers, they rarely, if ever, feel any pressure to choose one or the other. It's not a dilemma men can understand because it's not one they are presented with on a daily basis, as so many women are. But younger women are increasingly adopting that same attitude, refusing to choose, refusing to elevate one to a more important status than the other. "It's not a matter of choosing the global, 'What's more important, your family or your business?'" Kurtzig says. "I think you take each day." Both business and family, these successful women feel, are necessary to their happiness and fulfillment. To be successful at one, they need the other, and having both is possible, they emphasize.

"If you're a woman in business and you think you have to choose, I'm saying you don't," says Debbi Fields. The mother of three hopes to have more children, and plans to keep working. "I go crazy when I stay home," she says. "When I'm staying home, and just doing the kids and taking care of them, which is wonderful, I'm still not taking care of Debbi, which is Debbi the businesswoman. For me to feel good about myself, I have to feel I'm making a contribution for me, and a contribution for my family. I need that. I could not retire. I cannot stop working."

"If my children needed me, I'd always be there," says Kurtzig. "But it never was an issue. You have this guilt trip. I don't want to minimize the fact that I felt I should be home with the kids going to PTA meetings, and doing all those things other mothers were doing. I think everybody goes through this. It's part of the genes you have being a woman.

"But I had to be realistic. I would not be happy being home all day talking baby talk. My happiness and fulfillment is important. If I'm not happy, my kids are going to reflect that."

What their children may have lost in time shared, or attention given, they have probably made up for by having a fulfilled, not frustrated mother, these women say. Vigoda asked her children years ago if they would have preferred having a more traditional, stay-at-home mother. "I don't know whether they were being loyal or whether they were being truthful," she says, "but they said, 'Oh no, it's much more interesting to talk to you, and have you for a mother.'"

Kay Koplovitz doesn't have children, but she is just as equally unwilling to choose between her marriage and her career. "They're different things," she says. "It's the American way to say my marriage is more important. They're both important to me. I don't think you can say this is more important or that is more important. I know I will be an unhappy person if I can't do the things that I want to do. Therefore could my marriage survive my being a very unhappy person? Probably not."

True equality to these women is having the same freedom their male counterparts do—*to have a family and a professional life, without feeling guilty that one or the other is getting shortchanged.*

They acknowledge the special role conferred on the feminine sex through motherhood. "As long as women give birth to children, I think they'll always feel the need to be responsible and take care of them," says Ash.

At the same time, they also are acutely aware that there is no such expression today as "working father." The very idea of querying a male executive on how he juggles his roles of husband, father, and businessman, how he manages to "have it all," is ludicrous. They would like to make that question, and the term "working mother" equally invalid for women. But instead of trying to *change* the prevailing attitudes, these women are dedicated to learning to cope with them.

Some of them have made progress in reeducating their spouses to share, if not fully divide, chores. Diane Seelye Johnson says she had to explain how the washing machine worked to her husband after years of marriage, but now he is as likely to change the bedsheets as she is. Other women have solved those problems by hiring household help, so neither party has to do household chores.

But most surprising are the very successful women among this group who are married to very traditional men who not only do not divide the chores evenly, they don't lend a helping hand at all. Though these women wield great power at the office as the top executives of their own companies, some of them still play the role of the wife as secondary helpmate. They try to cope with it however, not change it.

Before Ash's husband died in 1980, her company had grown to amazing proportions. She routinely made multimillion dollar decisions at the office and oversaw a gargantuan network of employees and saleswomen. But in the sixteen minutes it took her to drive home from her office every day, she says she changed personaes, "from the chairman of the board to Mel Ash's wife."

"I had to make some drastic adjustments in order to be the person he wanted as a wife," Ash says. "He did not want a chairman of the board for a wife. He did not want me telling him what to do in any way, shape, or form. When I came home, he wanted me to be his wife, period."

And that's what she was. Despite the famous powder-puff pink image often associated with Ash, she is a nononsense, tough executive at the office. At home however, she says she was ". . . soft, and cooking for him, and 'sweetheart' and 'darling' and all that jazz. A good example of it is (the television program) *Cagney and Lacey*," Ash says. "When she [Lacey] goes home, she's a completely different person than she is when she's out screaming at the criminals."

Men such as Ash's late husband are not asked how they manage to "have it all" because they don't have to *do* it all, Ash says. "I used to sort of watch Mel and think to myself, 'For crying out loud.' I would go in and fix his breakfast and put it on the table. He would spend all the time I'd spent fixing breakfast, getting all dressed up, leaving his clothes all over the bathroom, leaving his shaving stuff all around, leaving everything in a mess. Then he would come in with his briefcase on his way out. He would eat his breakfast, say 'Have a good day, sweetheart, I will see you later,' and leave. Here the house was a mess, what's for dinner, call the plumber, see what happened to the swimming pool. All these things needed to be done. Then he would come home and say 'What's for dinner?'"

Though she knows it was an unfair distribution of responsibility, Ash says she accepted it because she knew her husband wanted a traditional wife, and she was willing to give him that.

Some might try to dismiss Ash's experience as being typical for women of her generation whose ideas of traditional male and female roles were not challenged. Most younger women generally want at least an indication of shared responsibility; yet some are as willing and accepting as Ash was of traditional roles in the home.

Debbi Fields for instance, at age thirty, is one of the youngest and most successful women entrepreneurs in the country. Despite her awesome business success, her ten-year marriage to Randy is as traditional as anything portrayed in the working-husband-stay-at-home-wife television households of the 1950s.

"I've always made certain that he is the king of the house," Debbi says, "that he is the one that is well taken care of."

It is a role she assumed gladly from the beginning of their relationship, and one that has not changed fundamentally despite major changes in their lifestyle. She assumes partial responsibility for the inequity of the situation, Fields says, because she spoils her husband, but she doesn't try to correct it.

Several years ago the Fields gave a dinner party for fifty guests. Debbi cooked all day long, and when the party was over, the house was a mess. "I turned to Randy and said, 'Would you help me with the dishes?'" she remembers. "He looked at me and said, 'Are you crazy? I hate to do dishes. I would never do dishes. Don't expect me to do dishes, ever. If you want these dinner parties, then I don't care what you do, but don't ever ask me [to help].'

"Basically it was my choice," Debbi says. "Either choose to have dinner parties, and be prepared to clean up and not complain, or have dinner parties, and have somebody else clean up."

She took that same approach when beginning her business, taking responsibility for preparing dinner, cleaning the house, and doing the yard work. Though Randy is a doting father, she also assumes primary responsibility for making sure their children are cared for. "I know what Randy expects," she says. "I just simply would never want him to watch the children and all those things. It's something I would never ask of him."

Randy says he made it clear from the start of their relationship that he wanted a traditional wife. "I'm not a househusband," he says. "There's not a househusband bone in my body. She's much more a traditional wife, which is interesting. I made it clear I was marrying a traditional wife. I didn't care what she did with her life, but in the house we would have a traditional man-woman [relationship]."

With the phenomenal growth of the business, the Fields have full-time help now, including a live-in nanny. But basic attitudes haven't changed, the Fields agree. "If I ask her to get me a cup of coffee, she gets me a cup of coffee," Randy says, "and I can't imagine she would ever ask me to get her one."

Debbi knows the situation is not an even division of duties, but says the extra load doesn't bother her. Both Randy and Debbi seem perfectly content with the roles they have chosen, and the resulting relationship. "You have to understand," she says. "I knew I wanted to create this business. I'd gone out and done something for Debbi that I believed in. Why should he suffer at home?"

Such traditional male-female role perceptions pose challenges for the single entrepreneurial woman as well. Personal relationships are often complicated for her because men may be intimidated by her success.

Since her husband's death six years ago, Ash says she has only been on a date three or four times. "Every time, the man seems to be threatened to high heaven by the fact my company does twenty times what his company does," she says.

Ellen Terry also says she doesn't have a hectic social life. "I date some, not a lot," Terry says. "I'm told the reason I don't is because first of all, I'm always working. But if I did make myself available, there would be many men who would still be threatened to take me out. To me that is ludicrous."

The problem of men feeling threatened by successful women is less of a problem today than in years past, says Stringer, but it still exists. "I've had men say, 'You're exciting, you're interesting,'—but no one wants it at home. They want it at the office, or at lunch, or in the evening, but not at home. I don't think you can change it. It is a stiff price, and a lot of times I've wondered was it worth it."

The question of whether it's worth it is, of course, a strictly personal one. These women are generally concerned with striking a balance in their lives, and like other questions, they would like to make the either/or question obsolete. Rather than asking the question or lamenting the answer, they would prefer to create an environment where it isn't relevant to ask.

Popcorn theorizes that many relationship problems could be solved if women would abandon the idea of marrying "up," or dating someone as successful, or more so, than they are. The idea that women should marry someone not just their equal but their superior in terms of business, is one of the most difficult traditions for even the most progressive women to leave behind.

"You know what the best partner for a successful woman is?" asks Popcorn. "A blue collar man. Those relationships work out well. They work out well because these guys are very self-confident in a very macho way. They know that they don't know a lot about, say style and polish, and they don't care that they don't know. They have an attitude that is very helpful. They sort of like themselves. That makes it possible for them to tolerate, to enjoy, get off on, a successful woman. But women do not reach down into those ranks."

"Reaching down" is something few women are willing to do, and it is probably even harder for successful entrepreneurial women, because they are self-made. Despite their adamant support for equality, not superiority, of one sex over the other, many of these successful women have accepted the traditional belief of "bettering" themselves through marriage. Considering the magnitude of the success those women have achieved, that's often appealing in theory, but practically impossible to execute.

"I always wanted someone I could look up to," says Stringer. "I always wanted to be married to an intelligent person. I never wanted to feel I was more successful."

Guisewite, who expects a relationship to include shared responsibilities, says men are not intimidated by her success because her comic strip displays her private anxieties on a daily basis. But despite logical approaches to the subject, her level of achievement poses relationship problems in her own mind.

"If I would get married, I feel it would have to be to someone at least as successful as I am," says Guisewite. "It's horrible. I think it's totally hypocritical because it seems in a way to sort of be acknowledging no progress. It's only taking the old situation of the man doing as well or slightly better, and escalating it up the income level."

But she adds honestly, "I need to have a great deal of respect for the person, and to me one of the things I respect is ambition."

*　　　　*　　　　*

The challenges posed by being a successful entrepreneurial woman are legion, whether they involve handling misconceptions in the board room, juggling an inordinate number of duties at home and the office, or coping with evolving personal relationships. They know it is a Herculean, almost impossible, task to "have it all," yet that's still what these women want—a successful career and a fulfilling home life. They know—perhaps better than anyone else—the demands placed on women today are unrealistic and unfair. Yet they don't let it bother them.

Are women asked to do too much? "Absolutely," says Debbi Fields. But she adds, in a statement typical of many of these women, "I never get into fairness. There are so many things in life that are not fair, that I never really question [it]. Addressing the fact that it's not fair is not really going to change the situation."

Despite the unrealistic expectations placed on members of their sex, these women also have little patience with those who use their gender as a reason for not succeeding in business.

"You can always look for excuses," says Kurtzig. "You can always look for hurdles. In whatever you do, you can find reasons why you can't succeed or do something, or you can take advantage of those handicaps. You can't change the fact that you're a woman so why make it an issue?" A feminist might point out the hurdles and handicaps she faced as a woman, but Kurtzig dismisses those. "I think you have hurdles in anything," she points out. "Nothing worth doing is easy. When I was in sales, if I didn't get the sale, I could say it was because I was a woman. That's a nice excuse."

"We all have advantages and disadvantages," says Kay Koplovitz. She has also refused to use her gender as an excuse. She chose to go into cable television because it represented the best route for a woman to succeed, but she never spent time lamenting over the other routes that were harder to navigate or effectively closed because of her sex.

"I never felt that way. I think it's wrong to feel that way. I would rather do something about it than waste my energy thinking about that."

The need to accept today's reality in order to go forward, versus wishing for tomorrow's potential utopia, explains the emphasis these women place on coping with unrealistic expectations rather than trying to change them. At some point in time, someone, somewhere, may have to tackle the issue of change directly, or the situation may always remain the same, with women assuming primary child care and household responsibilities in addition to professional duties. But these women are less concerned about that far off day than they are about coping with current reality. They spend little or no time worrying about the inequity of the situation, and are less interested in raising consciousness and changing the status quo, than they are with learning to handle it. Though they don't carry the banner of change, they nonetheless do effect it, in subtle ways, by their very success. For these women however it is an evolutionary, not a revolutionary process.

The battle cry for change that erupted in the '60s doesn't excite them. Instead of "change," the rallying call of the entrepreneurial woman of the 80s, is "cope."

But it is important to note that, despite the subtle or blatant discrimination these women have experienced, and the extra responsibilities they are expected to shoulder, they do not look upon their femininity as either a cross to bear, or a standard to wave. It is simply a fact to be accepted, a part of their being, which offers both the good with the bad, and the opportunity to make the best of it.

"I was aware of being a woman, I always have been," says Koplovitz, good-naturedly. "I kind of like being a woman. But I try to face reality. I never would allow myself to either internalize that, or to waste my energy—because it wasn't going to change. I was a woman. I was going to continue to be one."

Koplovitz and others like her are not going to waste their energies lamenting the fact that they are women. But while the basic fact may not change, the definition of being a woman has. Such women still strive to do it all, to be the competitive career woman, the ideal wife, and the model mother, but they no longer castigate themselves if they don't always fit those molds. The mere act of *trying* to do the impossible is enough for them, and they wisely, and healthily, realize that their goals will always exceed their grasp.

When Louise Vigoda first started her real estate development business, she dubbed her company Hera, after the Greek goddess of marriage, who is all things to all people. The decision was, she says, an unconscious one.

But as her professional duties increased, and she realized she needed to pierce the Superwoman myth and prioritize daily demands, the name took on ironic significance. When she became most frustrated at trying to "do it all," Vigoda says, she employed a new, effective "battle cry."

"I am not," Vigoda would point out, "Hera."

Different Strokes

"I don't do it the way men do. I do not
fight a battle, that if the attack doesn't
work that way, we'll go the other way. If
you listen to a man [form] a business plan,
it sounds like a war plan, like Eisenhower
and his generals. I don't have that same
approach. It's very hard to explain these
things. You do things the way you do, and
keep doing them."

*A*s a young home economics student, Diane Seelye
Johnson had to hem her tea towel four times before it was deemed acceptable by her teachers.

Later, as a junior in high school she enrolled in an
advanced algebra class. "There were thirty-one boys and
Diane," she remembers. "I stayed in the class for two days,
then I succumbed to the social pressure to get the hell out of
advanced algebra. It was the joke of the school, Diane and
the boys."

Still later, upon returning to college at age thirty-eight,
a counselor queried her about her field of study, asking
if she had decided to pursue nursing or teaching. When
Johnson told him she wanted to major in accounting, he
looked doubtful, and tried to dissuade her. "Oh, that's very
difficult," he warned, hoping she would take the hint.

"Good," Johnson replied shortly, "I need a challenge."

*   *   *

A decade or two of women in the work place has not changed centuries of tradition. And centuries of tradition dictate that women are more "nurturing" by nature than men, and so belong in "nurturing" professions, such as nursing, or teaching; not accounting or computer software, or cable television.

Whether it's because of tradition or natural inclination, there is no arguing that women do indeed dominate the so-called helping professions today. *There is also no denying that women generally approach business from a different, more caring, standpoint than men.* When joining large corporations for instance, statistics show women tend to gravitate toward the human oriented, personal areas, such as public relations and personnel. (It is interesting to note that senior corporate executives rarely come from that side of the business, as shown by the Korn/Ferry profile. Top executives historically begin their careers in finance/accounting and professional/technical departments.)

That tendency to enter nurturing professions also extends to women who start their own businesses. According to *Risk to Riches*, a report recently published by the Institute for Enterprise Advancement, women enter certain fields, those termed the helping or service industries such as cooking, cosmetics, fashion, clerical services, personnel, travel, catering, advertising and public relations, more frequently than others. The study reports that women-owned businesses comprise a substantial segment in these stereotypical "female" industries. For instance, women own 54.7 percent of all travel agencies, in contrast to their controlling 7 percent of the construction industry. They own 730,000 retail businesses, while owning only 21,000 energy-related businesses. Eating and drinking establishments accounted for $6.6 billion in women-owned business receipts in 1982, to the study, while receipts of women-owned businesses total a mere $135 million in electric and electronic firms.

The debate over whether women choose traditional "feminine" fields because those professions are more caring and the tendency to nurture comes naturally, or because they have been exposed to those fields by society, is of course endless. But based on the experience of these women, it seems to be a combination of the two. Women *are* more openly caring than men, and *have* been exposed more often to domestic pursuits. Because of that exposure, they are generally more comfortable in those and other related areas, and feeling at ease is essential to success in any endeavor. Thus it stands to reason women are going to enter fields they know best, and where they feel most at home, which for the time being still means traditionally female, nurturing careers.

However, when women are exposed to other fields, they gravitate toward those as well, indicating that women don't necessarily go into nurturing businesses simply because that's where their primary or sole interests lie. Those entrepreneurial women who were exposed to other nontraditional female fields, such as developer Louise Vigoda and oil field supply executive Diane Seelye Johnson, say they selected their businesses because they had observed family members with experience in those fields. In Vigoda's case, she grew up in a family that owned property, while Johnson's husband, her partner in the business, had spent his professional lifetime in the oil industry.

There may indeed be some inborn tendencies toward certain types of careers, as some experts theorize, but in the past, society has done little to influence other inclinations. Johnson for instance, says she might have pursued a nontraditional field years earlier if she had received some encouragement instead of feeling pressured to drop out of advanced math and stick to tea towels.

But whether it's attributable to an inborn bias or inadequate education, few women will argue that when it comes to the financial end of business, they don't automatically put the bottom line first as so many men do, and they are often uncomfortable dealing with finances in business.

Mary Kay Ash remembers when she was the only female member of the board of directors at a company where she worked. "There were seven men on the board," she recalls, "and every time I made a suggestion—remember now we were working with all women [sales force]—and every time I suggested something they would say, 'Mary Kay, you're thinking like a woman again.' I would think about how something they were going to do would affect the women. Not how it would affect the company, but how those women out there would react and feel about what they were going to do. I would interpret that for them, and they would say, 'Look, we've got to worry about the bottom line.'"

Worrying about the bottom line does not often come naturally for many of these women. On a personal level they are generally frugal, sensible money managers—Georgette Klinger for instance shakes her head in dismay at the idea of postponing bills until the due date, despite the theory of cash flow; and Sandra Kurtzig says she has a reputation for "counting pencils;" but these women and others derive little pleasure from corporate budgeting. They generally hire subordinates—most often men—to handle the financial end of their businesses, and many admit dealing with finances is often more difficult for women than it is for men.

That weakness can be easily overcome through study and training, but most of these women say even with that, they prefer and are strongest at the people aspect, the creative and inspirational end of their businesses. Fields motivates her staff through special contests, and makes a point of hiring people who share her philosophy of having fun at work. Terry offers annual prizes for top associates, and Mary Kay Cosmetics' seminars are legendary for their glamour. Ash says she decided to offer luxurious awards such as mink coats, pink Cadillacs, and diamonds, because she once received a fishing light as a sales prize. Ash practices "praising people to success," and through rousing speeches motivates associates to meet goals they never previously thought possible.

Her preference for the selling end of the business, and her dislike of the financial aspect, is the reason Ash's son Richard, who is now president and chief executive officer, joined his mother's company. Ash planned to start Mary Kay Cosmetics with the help of her husband. "I didn't know anything about administration," she admits. "To this day I don't know anything about it. I didn't know what you had to buy something for, what you had to sell it for to avoid going broke in between. I didn't know all these things. That was not my realm. I had never been in there, but my husband had, and I was going to let him handle that. I turned that over to him with the idea, 'that's your problem, don't worry me with it. I'm worrying about the important stuff over here, the color of these jars, and the manual, and hiring people.'"

Then a month before the company was to open for business, Ash's husband died of a heart attack.

In the midst of making funeral arrangements, her attorney and accountant advised her to take a financial loss and give up the idea of starting her own business. But Ash's savings were committed to the venture, so she felt as if she had no choice but to proceed with her plans, therefore she turned to her then twenty-year-old son for help. He left his job as an insurance agent, and went to work with his mother, who expected him to help "pick up boxes," and hopefully balance the books. If he had not, Ash says she would have hired someone else to do it. Though she is an intelligent, savvy businesswoman, finances simply don't appeal to her.

Lillian Katz says she forced herself to learn about finances when the staff she hired "almost destroyed the company." But she admits that that part of the business does not come naturally to her or to most women. "I don't know of any man that doesn't know the bottom line, do you?" Katz asks. "They understand the bottom line much more so than women. I think many women sometimes perceive finance as being unfeminine."

Though that may be a common perception, there's nothing unfeminine about managing money. If there is an innate weakness in that area on the part of women, just as men have certain strengths and weaknesses, it is nothing that can't be developed and improved, just as men can learn to be more nurturing. Unfortunately, it may take more time than some might like. According to *Risk to Riches*, the financial business as a whole is still one of the areas least influenced by the influx of women into the work force. In the twenty years since a woman first took a seat on the New York Stock Exchange, the female ranks have only grown to forty-eight. And, as a measure of their relative unimportance in that arena, the report points out, there is still no ladies' room in the luncheon club at the New York Stock Exchange.

Besides the types of professions women gravitate toward, and the weakness they exhibit in the financial area, no one can help but notice that women are changing to fit into the male dominated business world. Less noticeable is the fact that women are also having an impact, however slow or slight, on that world. New businesses have emerged to meet the needs of career women, such as daycare and maternity business clothes, for example. Employee benefits have also changed with the advent of women in the work force. Some companies now offer expanded maternity or parental leave; others help with the daycare dilemma, whether that be in the form of a referral service, or an on site facility; and in some companies, flexible hours or job sharing programs have been instituted.

Given these changes, there are still major differences in the way the two sexes approach business. Gender blindness may be the idealized goal in the business world, but gender equality is the actual goal. Few people think men and women take the same attitude toward doing business, and those who know what each sex can accomplish with their different strengths would not want a business world made up solely of either one or the other. Each sex possesses different attributes that complement each other, and make for a stronger whole.

Generally women are credited with bringing a more human approach to business. There are those who say if someone starts bleeding in an office, the women will rush around, calling for help, arranging to pay for hospital care, and ordering flowers. The men in the office on the other hand are more likely to move the victim off the carpet—to avoid paying cleaning costs, as they watch out for the almighty dollar.

Somewhere between the two extremes lies the truth about the different approaches men and women take toward business.

Ash remembers a prime example: the headquarters of Mary Kay Cosmetics today is a shiny metallic high-rise office building, towering on the edge of one of Dallas' busiest freeways. The eight-story building far outshines the low-rise offices the company had occupied for several years before, but in the early days of the company, those offices were considered palatial. "It was a beautiful step up for us," Ash says, remembering the old building fondly.

When the company had been in their new quarters for six months, Ash's son, Richard, asked his mother to drop by his office for a chat.

"I want to talk to you about the new building," Rogers told her.

"What about it?" Ash asked, looking around the office appreciatively.

"I don't mean this one," Rogers said. "I mean the *next* one."

"Richard," an exasperated Ash said, "the carpet's not even dirty yet, and you're talking about a new building?"

Ash shakes her head, still puzzled. "He was already talking five, ten years ahead," she says. "He was planning this building, when we just moved into the other one."

That's indicative of the pragmatic approach men take toward business. In general, men are rational, long-term planners, more concerned with profit and loss than women are, according to both popular theory and these entrepreneurial women.

"If you told me I had to build the Golden Gate bridge, I would just jump off of it," Ash declares. "I wouldn't know where to start. But men say okay, and start getting some plans together."

The female entrepreneur is more apt to rely heavily on intuition, express more concern about employees and customers, and respond flexibly to situations as they occur. These women don't label those traits as weaknesses however; they applaud them.

"I don't do it the way men do," says Lillian Katz proudly. "I do not fight a battle, that if the attack doesn't work that way, we'll go the other way. If you listen to a man plan a business plan, it sounds like a war plan, like Eisenhower and his generals. I don't have that same approach. It's very hard to explain these things. You do things the way you do, and keep doing them."

"I think women in general are a little more touch and feel in their business relationships," says Kay Koplovitz. "I mean that in a positive way. I think it's a positive. I think women try to make concensus decisions, and to be sympathetic to more than one point of view, which I think is a strength."

That ability to trust their instincts is especially apparent in entrepreneurial women. While men may be able to explain the whys and wherefores of their actions, pointing to in depth analyses and marketing studies for backup, many of these women are uncomfortable when asked to explain their actions and decisions. "I don't stop and analyze," says Ellen Terry. "I'm a very intuitive person. I hire intuitively." Potential employees may take tests when applying at Terry's agency, but she says she doesn't necessarily heed them, choosing instead to rely on her instinct. "I think women listen to their intuition more than men as a general rule," Terry says.

Just as these women normally did not make out long-range plans, following their intuition instead, they also attack immediate needs with more common sense than business administration training. When Paula Stringer opened her real estate offices, her company was considered innovative because she upgraded the yard signs placed in front of properties. The move was not made as the result of an in depth marketing survey or because Stringer was consciously trying to set herself apart from the competition. "I like nice surroundings," she says simply. "I wanted to have yard signs that reflected my personality."

Similarly, the pink containers used for Mary Kay Cosmetics, introduced in 1963, have become the basis for Ash's association with pink as a signature color. Though subsequent studies have shown the color pink has a calming, soothing effect, Ash did not make the selection based on anyone's suggestion or expertise. She chose the color because she felt the product would look good next to traditional white bathroom tiles.

There is also nothing particularly mysterious or calculated in Louise Vigoda's approach to building management. When she assumed control of a new project, Vigoda says she employed simple common sense, not specialized marketing or management techniques. "I attacked it on a practical, sensible basis," she says. "When I went into the women's restroom and it smelled, I knew it wasn't good. When it was ugly, it wasn't good. I just said, 'Look we have a problem.' I'm very good at problem solving. If you are willing to work and have a brain in your head, and apply it to the problem, I think you're going to go the distance."

The ability of these women to "go the distance," by relying on their instinct has not been lost on male executives, some women say. "Businessmen today are beginning to understand to trust their guts," says Debbi Fields, "while women automatically trust their intuition."

Perhaps the tendency to trust their intuition instead of planning long range, explains why these women generally are not conscious empire builders. Some of them not only did not plan a major business venture, they actively resisted the idea.

Fields, for instance, did not want to open a second store, even when her first shop was well established. Friends advised her to expand but she refused, not out of concern that the bottom line would suffer, but because of worry that poor quality and the lack of her own personal touch might disappoint her customers. She finally approved expansion plans, only after ascertaining that quality controls could be put into effect.

Once an empire like Mrs. Fields has developed, it is also interesting to note these women are not particularly concerned about keeping it in the family. The idea of handing their carefully nurtured business down from generation to generation, as men have done for years, is not a major concern. Many of these women have children who have joined the company, including Ash, Johnson, Katz, Stringer, and Klinger, but generally they say they refrained from pressuring their offspring to do so. They were more concerned that their children find their own niche in business, than that the company remain under family management. Family dynasty building was not an aim, or a strategy, but a byproduct of their own spontaneous success.

"I never really discussed it or had it in mind," says Klinger of her daughter Kathryn's decision to join the company. "Because I am an individual, I expected her to do exactly what she wanted. In her yearbook, someone wrote, 'Kathryn is going to go into her mother's business.' I was very surprised." Kathryn joined the company in 1970 and now serves as president.

Some women not only do not care whether their children join their venture, they worry about the pressures their children feel to achieve a similar measure of success in any endeavor—which would be difficult at best. Vigoda says that because both she and her husband have achieved a substantial measure of success in their respective fields, and a high profile in the local community, her children have suffered from the pressure of other people's expectations. Terry also notes that her children sometimes feel intimidated by her professional accomplishments. "They look at me as extremely successful," she says, "where I see I've had many more failures, in my mind, than I've had successes."

Though the Fields' children are still under the age of ten, Debbi and Randy have already taken steps to deal with any pressure they may feel to live up to their parents' career achievements. The Fields have set up different businesses, such as a gift shop, a clothing store, and another cookie company, named after each of their children, to give them something of their own. "I don't want them to feel like they have to follow my footsteps," Debbi says.

That concern for people's feelings often extends beyond the family to include employees and customers. Many successful entrepreneurial women note that the feminine sex is naturally more sensitive to the needs of others than are their male counterparts. While some experts theorize that this caring tendency limits the professional potential of women, because it can translate into a desire to be liked at the cost of smart business decisions, these women feel being sensitive to employees' feelings makes for a happier, more productive, and thus more profitable, company. For many of them that means providing warm little touches, such as the birthday cards Ash sends to employees, or more major considerations, such as improved maternity benefits. But often it simply means expressing a sense of caring on a daily basis.

Debbi Fields notices the different approach from the minute she and Randy enter their building, where they office across from each other while maintaining separate businesses. "Randy and I have two different, very distinct, views on how a company should be run," she says. "Randy's communication is very different from my communication. He is absolutely matter of fact, and I am very concerned about what I am going to say, how the person will take it. I'm very concerned about leaving them intact so they feel very successful. Randy is very insensitive to not knowing that somebody's down or depressed. I can just walk through and see somebody's eyes and say, 'Do you have a problem? Do you want to talk to me?'"

A caring approach is one of the best qualities these women bring to the business world. They are genuinely concerned about their employees, but they are equally concerned with running an efficient business. They firmly believe that contented employees are more productive, and more productive staff members make a more profitable company. And the success of their respective companies shows that philosophy to be more than just happy talk.

Because the business world is still an arena dominated by men, and likely to remain so for the foreseeable future, these women say female executives are more likely to adapt, than effect change in their surroundings. Business is a bigger and more established entity than women as a group are in the work place. But as more and more women open businesses, perhaps in seven to nine decades, they may become a dominant force in the business world and find themselves the rulemakers. "When you're bigger you can affect them," says Faith Popcorn. "Usually David doesn't win. Goliath wins."

Right now the business world is toughening women up professionally, more than women are softening it up. Learning about finance and how to plan for long-range growth, for instance, help women fit in to that male dominated world. That's not to say however that the impact of women is nonexistent. There is a mutual exchange taking place because men are also beginning to learn about intuition and sensitivity. That change is simply more gradual and less noticeable than the changes women are undergoing.

The toughening up of women professionally doesn't have to come at the cost of femininity, these women point out. Women have passed that stage of being imitation men, and they recognize that being business smart doesn't mean being unfeeling. Instead, a sharp business edge should enhance those qualities women already bring to the board room. "If you took all the women off this earth for thirty years, it would go to pot," Ash says. "We inject the sensitivity, the compassion, the love if you will, the whatever it is that makes life. We add the flowers in the room."

Ellen Terry owns a book entitled *Think Like a Man, Act Like a Lady, Work Like a Dog.* The title may have served as appropriate advice in the past, but there's a subtle difference in the way these women have approached their work. As they look back on their careers, the most significant point is that while they do act like ladies and work like dogs, they've obviously learned to think like men *and* women, using their minds, their intuition, and their femininity to their advantage.

For these super-successful entrepreneurs, what is feminine and what is not is rarely a conscious concern. They are self-confident enough not to worry about femininity. They do what comes naturally, whether that means listening to their instincts when making decisions, or making an extra effort to create a family atmosphere for their employees, knowing that their company will thrive because of it.

"I don't know what 'femininity' is," says Diane Seelye Johnson, former four-time tea towel hemmer. "I like what [Congresswoman] Patricia Schroeder said one time, [when asked] 'What is a nice girl like you doing on an Armed Forces Committee?' She said, 'Well, I was born with a brain and a uterus—and I've made use of both of them.'"

No Fear of Failure

"You need to explore the possibilities and find out what kind of negotiations will work—to *not take no for an answer*."

*D*ebbi Fields opened her first cookie store, originally entitled Mrs. Fields Chocolate Chippery, with a $50,000 bank loan, a supply of soft, chewy cookies, and a bet with her husband Randy, who predicted she wouldn't sell $50 worth of cookies the first day. She opened for business at noon, and in the first few hours it looked as if Randy would win the bet. "I had all these cookies," she says, "all these dreams, visions, aspirations. What happened was I didn't have a single customer."

Not many people came in to see the new shop, and those who did were taken aback at the cookies' twenty-five cent selling price. Cookies at nearby bakeries sold for nine cents. "I didn't make a single sale," Debbi says. "By two o'clock I was getting so depressed. I was thinking, 'Okay, everybody told me I was going to fail, it looks real obvious that's going to happen to me.'"

But before she accepted defeat, Fields wanted to make sure it was the concept that failed, not Debbi Fields herself. "I can accept that," she says, "but before I do, I want to make sure I can say I did everything. I never want to close the book on history and say, 'You know, if I'd only. . . .' I

always run into people who tell me, 'You know if I'd
only. . . .'"

Determined not to quit, she piled the cookies on a bak-
ing sheet, locked the store and walked up and down the
street, giving them away. Like children following the Pied
Piper, paying customers soon trailed her back to the store.
By the end of the day, Fields had won the bet with her
husband.

Debbi Fields was twenty years old when she opened that
first store, and older, experienced business people had
strongly discouraged her from pursuing the idea. Though
friends always raved about the chocolate chip cookies she
baked in her California kitchen, they were skeptical when
she mentioned her plan to sell them commercially.

"Every one of them told me I was going to fail," Fields
says, "that it was a stupid idea."

Even Randy, while encouraging her to try, and cosign-
ing the bank loan, admits he never expected the venture to
succeed. "It was inconceivable it could be successful,"
Randy Fields says, ticking off the reasons why. "Eighty-five
percent of businesses fail. Nobody was in the soft, chewy
cookie business. All the market studies said nobody would
buy them. She didn't know anything about business."

Despite the dire prognostications, Debbi was unde-
terred. The possibility that the venture might not succeed
didn't bother her. "When people said, 'Debbi you're going
to fail,' I said, 'Gosh, is that the worst thing that can happen?'" She tested the idea mentally by envisioning the worst
case scenario: "I'm going to go into the cookie business and
lose the $50,000. I'd have to figure out a way to pay it back.
I'm willing to do that."

Fields' lack of fear at the prospect of failure, and her
refusal to accept it, is not just an indication of stubbornness,
but a hallmark of successful entrepreneurial women. Many
of these women faced similar problems when starting their

companies, but *they refused to accept temporary defeats as permanent failures.*

"When you're down in a tunnel, you can either hide your head or start digging out," says Ellen Terry. Like Fields, Terry is also doggedly persistent. When Terry decided to make real estate her career, she told the agency employment representative that she needed a draw against commission of $1,000 a month to support herself. That wasn't done, she was told. Terry had no credentials and no experience, but she insisted she be given a draw to support herself. After two more interviews the company agreed to give her a $500 draw for six months.

For Terry and other entrepreneurial women, not succeeding, whether at selling that first batch of cookies or when requesting a draw against commission, was simply not an option. "Failure," says Terry, "never entered my mind."

Each of these women possesses an ability to discount roadblocks, which is typical of their approach when faced with any adversity. They view problems as challenges, not obstacles, as occasional detours or delays, but never as dead ends. Some suggest that this optimistic resilience may spring from the female experience. Because women often have had to struggle to reach their goals, they may be more accustomed to setbacks, more able to handle adversity through familiarity with it. "Women have a higher tolerance for pain," reminds Faith Popcorn. "They can take anything. That's what makes them so fabulous."

Interestingly, many of these women often refer to themselves, cheerfully, proudly, and accurately, as "fighters." They become animated at the very thought of rising to a challenge.

"The more difficult it is, the more there is to fight for," says Georgette Klinger. "I'm not giving up so easily in life. If I had given up, I wouldn't be here. I'm a fighter."

Psychological compensation is one of the rewards of a

challenge, says Kay Koplovitz. "I'm one of those people for whom 'being there' is not important, 'getting there' is everything. The getting there is more important. Not that I don't enjoy a good life, but I like to be in the battle . . . I think all my life I'll be getting somewhere. That's what I enjoy."

The relish for a challenge, the adamant refusal to accept failure, and the corresponding willingness to embrace risks, may be the reason that entrepreneurs have caught the imagination of modern day America. Those who place a premium on security and hate the idea of wondering where next month's rent is coming from, average men and women, are endlessly fascinated by the courageous few who willingly trade the safe and certain for the risky and unknown.

The current fascination with entrepreneurs may be due, in part, to timing. After the economic ravages of the Depression, followed by the emotional strain and sacrifices of World War II, Americans elevated the corporation to an unprecedented level of respect. Success in the 1950s, 1960s, and 1970s was measured in terms of security, an ability to provide the basic necessities on a guaranteed basis, and that was best done in the framework of the big business corporation. Self-employment was not considered the key to success, but being an "organization man" was. In the '70s, admiration for the "organization man" evolved into a passion for creative, inspirational management—but still within the corporate framework. Only in recent years, possibly as affluence and security have become taken for granted by generations with only dim memories or no firsthand knowledge of difficult times, has risk-taking become fashionable again.

The interest in entrepreneurs as modern day heroes is slightly puzzling to these entrepreneurial women. While they are intellectually aware of the risks they took, they seem emotionally oblivious to them. "I *wanted* something that was dependent on me," says Terry. "That the harder I worked, the more chances for gain." These women eagerly accept the element of risk, but at the same time they minimize it by plainly refusing to fail. *For these women, taking a business risk is no gamble when the person they're betting on is themselves.* They are puzzled by women who prefer security with limitations, to risk with potential for great reward. A guaranteed paycheck every two weeks, with at best predictable possibilities for advancement or salary increases, holds little appeal for them, despite the uncertainty posed by running their own businesses.

Entrepreneurs find venturing out without the shelter of an organization exhilarating, not frightening. For these supremely confident individuals, self-employment is not a tenuous twig to cling to, but a lifesaving rope, that dangles unlimited opportunity within their reach.

That's how Mary Kay Ash viewed it. She was thrilled to leave a steady job waiting tables in her mother's restaurant for $11 a week, for a commission-only selling job. "I didn't see it as a risk," she says. "I saw it as an opportunity to do something I couldn't do in any other job. As a waitress, I could make $11 a week forever."

Like other entrepreneurial women, Ash never considered the possibility she might not succeed. "I decided it was going to work or else," she says. "I just never even thought about the fact it would fail. That was not a possibility."

The possibility of failure is easier to discount when starting out, says Sandra Kurtzig, because there is little at stake. Like many businesses started by women, Kurtzig's company was started on a limited budget with no heavy debt to pay back. "I think you get more conservative as you get a few dollars," Kurtzig says. "When you have nothing to lose, it's easy to be a risk-taker. Fifty percent of zero is still zero. You can lose 100 percent of zero and not be any worse off. When you have nothing and you're still eating hamburgers, it's fine. It's once you're eating steak you tend to take a little less risk."

*   *   *

The success these women have achieved is attributable to their self-confidence, their ability to manage and inspire people within and outside their companies, and their willingness to work what Ash calls "hard and smart." People who don't succeed, according to many of these women, either didn't want to pursue their dream badly enough to put in the long hours and hard work required, or they didn't learn as they went along.

In building their companies, before they became business success stories, these women have all put in more than their share of eighteen-hour days and seven-day weeks. Debbi Fields remembers being so tired the first few months in business that she considered selling her share of the fledgling business to a friend. When Kurtzig started ASK, "I did everything," she says. "I did the programs. I sold them. I wrote the invoices. I collected the money. I deposited the money. I wrote all the paychecks out. I did the taxes. I did everything. I turned off the lights at night. Sometimes the lights didn't get turned off at night because we worked all night." And though Mary Kay Cosmetics' seminars are glamorous affairs today, the first gala dinner for 200 was cooked by the company founder, right down to deboning the chicken.

While women are rarely at a loss for the high energy levels required for successful entrepreneurism—possibly because of the experience they gain from juggling so many different roles—there is more to being successful than working hard. Some women don't always maximize their efforts, these women note.

"Sometimes they work hard, but not smart," says Ash. "There is a difference. You can go out there and dig a ditch from daylight until dark and not get anywhere."

"Working smart" includes learning from mistakes. These women point out that they are not unfamiliar with failure. Most of them have experienced failure in varying degrees at one time or another, but they use it as a learning experience and try to avoid repeating the error. Though they generally hate to lose at anything, most of them don't attach a stigma to failure. They view it as a learning opportunity encountered on the way to success. People sometimes joke that you're not considered an entrepreneur until you've had one solid failure to your name. Considering the sobering statistics that show most new businesses don't survive, much less flourish over the long run, that's probably a wise approach to take. But if a business does fail, a true entrepreneur will rebound quickly and start over again, undaunted by what she considers a temporary setback.

Because these women have put in more than forty-hour weeks, because they have poured every ounce of their energy and their selves into their companies, these businesses are more than just jobs or a way to make a living. But while a great portion of their identities are often tied up in their companies, these women generally are not classic "workaholics," with few or no outside interests. They may have gone through periods requiring single-mindedness bordering on obsession, but once the company has reached a certain level of success, they often cut back their hours. Though the cutback may be from eighty hours a week to sixty, it *does* represent a decrease, a willingness to step back.

Most of these women are interested in being more than consummate business executives. They want to be whole people, with full lives, at and away from the office. Though they enjoy their work immensely, and derive tremendous fulfillment from it, their identities don't seem as dependent on their companies as are the identities of many male executives—perhaps because they're rarely allowed the luxury of such an exclusive focus.

"I never was just a businesswoman," Georgette Klinger says. "I always said, if anybody ever recognizes me as such, that's the time I'd get out."

Maintaining some sort of balance is a constant battle, but these women pride themselves on their ability to do so. Most of them vacation regularly and have numerous outside interests apart from business. "I very determinedly, jealously, guard my time off now," says Koplovitz. "There are so many impositions on my time, I'm very jealous about saving my time to play tennis, to work out . . . I take about four weeks vacation every year. I believe in regenerating mental attitudes. My mind is always thinking. It doesn't shut off."

Also refreshing to note is that while they are justifiably proud of and heavily involved with their companies, these women rarely place business over personal relationships in level of importance.

When Sandra Kurtzig told someone her children's ages incorrectly, and called one son by the wrong name, she realized it was time to reassess her work load. The business was beginning to encroach on her personal life, including time spent with her children, which was the reason she became an entrepreneur in the first place. "After fourteen years, I said, 'hey those kids are really cute,'" Kurtzig says, laughing. "They're fun. I want to spend more time with them." She decided it was time to make some adjustment and start enjoying what she had worked so hard to attain. She took a sabbatical first, then 'retired' as CEO, retaining the title of chairman.

Those who strive for such balance, those who want to have it all, at the office and at home, have been called "lifestyle entrepreneurs," people who enjoy, but do not live solely for their businesses. Despite the difficulties of starting a business, and the hardships of running it, despite the constant claims on their time and attention, most of these women speak of their climb to the top fondly. They give the impression that coping with difficulties and setbacks, juggling several roles at once, is done with ease. When pressed, they admit it wasn't that way at all, but there is little sense of the anguish of struggle in their stories. "I don't stop to think about it," says Terry. "I just *do* it. I'm a very action oriented person. If something needs to be done, I just do it. I don't sit back and think, 'Gosh, how am I going to juggle this?' I just do it."

Just as these women do not analyze how they got where they are, they also do not spend much time reflecting on their failures or successes. They know they have achieved an unusually high degree of professional accomplishment, whether it's measured in terms of dollars, titles, fame, or achievement, and they are proud of that; but they don't pat themselves on the back too often. Instead, they heartily embrace the adage of success being a journey, not a destination, and constantly push themselves to go higher. "No one ever feels they have arrived," says Louise Vigoda. "Every end is only a means to another end. You think, 'Oh boy, if this happens everything will be wonderful.' But then when this happens, you think of something else."

Success to these women is always just beyond their grasp. "I'm just about to make it," Faith Popcorn says. "There's always going to be some place to go. If this company's name were a household word worldwide, I would have made it. IBM has made it. That's what I call making it."

Whether they ever "make it" to the extent of IBM, their tremendous success in business has already altered their way of life irrevocably. The demands on their time are greater, and their standard of living is higher, but these women say it hasn't changed their basic personalities. They have always been confident, and for the most part, they don't let themselves become cocky. "I still have a hard time thinking of myself as successful," says Kurtzig. "Estee Lauder is successful. Katharine Graham is successful. I'm just me. I'm no different."

Whether they feel particularly successful or not, they are perceived that way by others. And that perception can often be used to great advantage. One of the aspects Kurtzig and other women like best about reaching the measure of success they have, is the platform it affords them to have an influential voice with which to give back to the community. Perhaps it's the nurturing tendency cropping up again, but many of these women spend a great deal of their energy working with community programs in a variety of areas. Many of them also put the force of their companies behind community needs, such as the information on missing children which appears on Mrs. Fields' cookie bags, or Lillian Vernon's corporate support of a marathon supporting education programs for the handicapped.

"Dollars are a part of success but I don't think they're the only criteria," says Koplovitz. "I think that your ability to influence policy, your ability to lead people, your contributions back into society if you will, or to individuals in society, to help make the environment better, to help make somebody's life better—those kinds of things are all measures of success to me."

Despite their success and their efforts to serve the community, many of these women are surprised and a little uneasy to find themselves in the position of role model.

Kurtzig says she used to hate the suggestion that she was a role model, but she's accepted the notion in recent years. As her community leadership role increases, it no longer bothers her. "I guess that's sort of the mellowing of my mind," she says, "where I realize . . . I can be an inspiration. I guess I really do get kind of excited, if I can help women see that they can do it, that there's nothing unique about what I've done, that you can do it, go for it."

Go for it, and keep one thing in mind, Debbi Fields says: no is an unacceptable answer. Successful entrepreneurs apply that philosophy in everything, from major obstacles to incidentals. When Fields is faced with a seemingly unsolvable problem at work, she will shut people in a room and refuse to let anyone leave until a solution is reached. She demonstrates that same persistence to solve the minor irritants of travel.

"I call up room service," she explains, "and I say, 'I know that it says room service isn't available until 7 o'clock, however I need to have coffee at 6. Is that a possibility?'" When the answer is no, as it usually is, Fields then calls the assistant manager, or if necessary, the general manager. "Hi Manager," she says. "I'm only the customer and I want to know what possibilities exist to have you deliver coffee to my room at 6 o'clock, since your room service isn't available until 7?"

She has not yet failed, Fields says triumphantly, to get coffee before 7. "You need to explore the possibilities," she says, "and find out what kind of negotiations will work—to *not take no for an answer.*"

EPILOGUE

"The point you really need to come to is
that anybody can do it."

*E*ntrepreneurs are the new American heroes, and
women are leading the march of that heroic force. In
the process, they are revolutionizing the way America works in the business world and at home. My purpose in
writing *Self-Made Women* was to find out what if anything
sets them apart from other businessmen and women.

Much to my surprise, the twelve women I interviewed
often echoed Sandra Kurtzig's comment that they weren't
any different, that the incredible level of success they have
reached, running multi-million dollar companies created
out of thin air and high hopes, could be matched by anyone
willing to work hard and dream big.

In some respects they are right. For the most part these
entrepreneurs, among the most successful businesswomen
in America, are very much like the coworker in the next
office, or the neighbor down the street. As children, they
weren't necessarily stellar students, or particularly ambitious adolescents. As adults they still, to borrow an expression, put their pantyhose on one leg at a time. Kay Koplovitz
may be a top television executive, but she notes that her
parents still expect her to do the dishes when she goes
home. Debbi Fields may run a company of international
scope, but she says she's still the same person who struggled through school. And Sandra Kurtzig may be a computer software wizard, but she points out she still has to
wait in line at the post office. Like women everywhere they
fret over their appearance, worry about their children, and

keep an eye on their budgets, although those budgets admittedly have more zeroes after the dollar sign than most.

But while such modest admissions may be refreshing and encouraging to hear, in many ways I think these women sell themselves short when they downplay their uniqueness. They are, to borrow another expression shamelessly, different from you and I. Their very accomplishments, do indeed make them special people. Lots of women work hard and dream big, but their businesses never make it out of the second bedroom where they started. And what these women have done, while starting super-successful companies, is begin to effect a quiet change in the business world that will eventually affect us all profoundly.

While everyone at one time or another fantasizes about starting their own company, about being not just the CEO but the genius behind a hugely successful business, few take steps to implement the dream. And even fewer do it successfully.

What I have found in interviewing these twelve remarkable women is that through some unquantifiable chemistry, possibly just their particular life experience, they have primed themselves to become willing listeners to the siren call of entrepreneurship.

What successful entrepreneurial women are made of are the qualities many of these women share in abundance: a healthy dose of self-confidence; a high energy level that impels them to work hard at everything they do; a goal-oriented personality; and a willingness to take risks, knowing that those risks can be minimized by betting on what they know best—themselves.

It is inspiring to note that these women prove successful entrepreneurship does not call for sacrificing one's personal life or one's femininity. These women prove that the balancing act between home and career can be done successfully, if you are willing to admit that Superwoman is a pleasant myth. Ironically, because they are perfectionists, they keep striving to make that myth a reality; thankfully they maintain their sanity by refusing to castigate themselves when they don't quite make that happen. In addition these women take not only risks but responsibility, and by doing so, they prove you don't have to wear a three piece suit and be a locker room buddy to do so successfully. They may be considered the epitome of feminism, but they are more accurately the epitome of femininity in the best sense, tempering strength with caring, profit making ability with intuition, and appeal with intelligence. They don't talk about equal rights because they assume they have them, and if they're not given those rights unconditionally, their ultimate performance demands them. Some may see such flexibility as a step backward; to me it represents a giant step forward. These women, pioneers of sorts, have ceased thinking of themselves as "women entrepreneurs" and think of themselves as entrepreneurs, period. They want the same things men do: a successful professional and personal life of their own making. They're not going to take no for an answer; and by doing so, they're changing the way others, particularly men, perceive them.

The unusual blend they possess of persistence, perspective, caring, business savvy, and balanced ambition is unique to a very few.

It's no wonder these women are phenomenally successful. They act while others think. They see opportunities where others see only peril. And they take it one day at a time, performing as common sense, intuition, and intelligence dictate.

Think entrepreneurial women aren't unique people? Think again.

SOURCES

The Corporate Woman Officer. Heidrick and Struggles. 1986

Korn/Ferry International's Executive Profile: A Survey of Corporate Leaders in the Eighties. 1986

Inside Corporate America. Allan Cox

Risk to Riches Women and Entrepreneurship in America A Special Report. Edie Fraser, Editor. Institute for Enterprise Advancement 1986.

ABOUT THE AUTHOR

Diane Jennings is a "High Profile" writer for the *Dallas Morning News*. Before joining the staff of the News, she worked at the Southwest Bureau of *Women's Wear Daily* and *W*.

SUSAN J. DOUGLAS is the Catherine Neafie Kellogg Professor of communication studies at the University of Michigan. She is author of *Where the Girls Are: Growing Up Female with the Mass Media* and *Inventing American Broadcasting, 1899–1922*. She has written for *The Nation, The Village Voice, Ms., The Progressive, In These Times*, and the *Washington Post*. *Listening In* won the Hacker Prize in 2000 for the best popular book about technology and culture.